NURSERY KNITS

NURSERY KNITS

TESSA WATTS-RUSSELL

OCTOPUS BOOKS

Publishers Note

Knitting Notes

Abbreviations: these are listed in the Knitting Know-how section on page 131.

Substituting alternative yarns: it is always advisable to use the yarn specified in the pattern. Yarn spinners' and stockists' addresses are given on page 142. If, however, you find it necessary to substitute an alternative yarn, purchase only one ball at first and knit a large tension square to make sure that the yarn is suitable for the pattern and that it produces results with which you will be satisfied.

The Designers

The majority of the designs in this book were created by Tessa Watts-Russell.
Additional material created by:
Rosanne Bartlett and Marjorie Moore of Blackberry Design (Christmas Trees page 119, Pockets Top page 50, Balloons page 46)
Pearl Crook (Playtime page 90)

Annabel Fox (Big Top page 29)
Margaret Lambert of Sirdar Hand-knitting Yarns (Monday's Child page 55, Sugar and Spice page 21)
Debbie Scott for Patons (Bears in the Wood page 100, Easter Chicks page 10, Noël Noël page 111, Going Dotty page 58).

First published 1987 by
Octopus Books Limited
59 Grosvenor Street
London W1

© 1987 Octopus Books Limited

ISBN 0 7064 2853 6

Produced by Mandarin Publishers Limited
22a Westlands Road
Quarry Bay
Hong Kong

Printed in Hong Kong

CONTENTS

Real rabbits are soft to touch, and so are the fluffy white Easter bunnies on these grey slipovers. Because the bunnies are knitted in soft angora the slipovers deserve careful hand-washing.

SPRING FEVER

When spring is in the air it means off with the old winter woollies and into lighter, cooler knitwear. Ducklings and bunnies are favourite spring themes and they are here in abundance, along with Easter chicks, a frog and jumpers without motifs but using different stitch effects – some traditional, some new and all in fresh spring shades of medium to lightweight yarns.

EASTER BUNNIES

Simple, yet adorable slipovers for child and teddy.

MEASUREMENTS
Child's slipover
To fit chest 46(51,56) cm [18(20,22) in]
Actual measurements 51(56,61) cm
Length to shoulders 25·5(28,30·5) cm
Teddy's slipover
To fit chest 38 cm [15 in]

MATERIALS
Child's slipover
2(2,3) × 50 g balls King Cole 4 ply Superwash in main colour A
1 × 20 g ball Woolgatherer's Radiangor 2 ply in contrast colour B
Teddy's slipover
2 × 50 g balls King Cole 4 ply Superwash in main colour A
1 × 20 g ball Woolgatherer's Radiangor 2 ply in contrast colour B
A pair each of 2 mm (No 14) and 3 mm (No 11) knitting needles

TENSION
32 sts and 40 rows to 10cm measured over st st

NOTE
The contrast colour yarn B is used double throughout.

INSTRUCTIONS FOR CHILD'S SLIPOVER

BACK

★ Using 2 mm needles and A, cast on 81(89,97) sts.
Rib row 1: K1, ✲ P1, K1, rep from ✲ to end.
Rib row 2: K2, ✲ P1, K1, rep from ✲ to last st, K1.
Rep these 2 rows for 2·5(2·5,4) cm, ending rib row 2. ★
Change to 3 mm needles.
Work in st st until back measures 11·5(14,15·5) cm
from beg, ending with a P row.
  ★★ **Shape armholes**
Next row: K4 sts and slip these sts onto a safety-pin,
K to end.
Next row: P4 sts and slip these sts onto a safety-pin,
P to end: 73(81,89) sts.
Next row: K2, K2 tog, K to last 4 sts, K2 tog tbl, K2.
Next row: P2, P2 tog tbl, P to last 4 sts, P2 tog, P2.
Rep the last 2 rows until 57(65,73) sts remain.
Next row: K2, K2 tog, K to last 4 sts, K2 tog tbl, K2.
Next row: P.
Rep these 2 rows until 49(57,65) sts remain, ending
with a P row. ★★
Work straight until back measures 24(26·5,29) cm
from beg, ending with a P row.
Shape neck
Next row: K6(10,14), K2 tog, K2, turn and leave
remaining sts on a spare needle.
Dec 1 st at neck within the 2 st border until
6(10,14) sts remain.
Cast off.
Return to sts on spare needle.
With right side facing, slip first 29 sts onto a holder,
rejoin yarn and complete to match first side of neck,
reversing all shaping.

FRONT

Work as given for back from ★ to ★.
Change to 3 mm needles.

Work in st st until front measures 22 rows less than
back to armholes, ending with a P row.
Work motif from chart as follows:
Row 1: K22(26,30)A, 8B, 5A, 3B, 5A, 3B, 5A, 8B,
22(26,30)A.
Row 2: P22(26,30)A, 6B, 6A, 3B, 7A, 3B, 6A, 6B,
22(26,30)A.
Continue in this way, working from chart until row 22
has been completed.
Now work armhole shaping as given for back from
★★ to ★★.
Shape neck
Next row: K14(18,22), K2 tog tbl, K2, turn and leave
remaining sts on a spare needle.
Continue to dec 1 st within the 2 st border at neck
edge on every row until 6(10,14) sts remain.
Work straight until front measures same as back to
shoulder, ending with a P row.
Cast off.
Return to sts on spare needle.
With right side facing, slip first 13 sts onto a holder,
rejoin yarn and complete to match first side of neck,
reversing all shaping.

NECKBAND

Join left shoulder seam.
With right side facing and using 2 mm needles and
A, pick up and K4 sts down right back neck, K across
29 sts from back neck holder, pick up and K3 sts up
left back neck and 36(36,40) sts down left front neck,
K across 13 sts from front neck holder, then pick up
and K36(36,40) sts up right front neck: 121(121,
129) sts
Beg with rib row 2, work 17 rows in rib as given for
back. Cast off.

ARMBANDS

Join right shoulder and neckband seam.
With right side facing and using 2 mm needles and
A, pick up and K109(109,117) sts evenly round
armhole including the 4 sts at each end on safety-
pin.
Complete as given for neckband.

TO MAKE UP

Join side and armband seams. Fold rib bands in half
to wrong side and slipstitch into place. Press lightly
following instructions on ball band.

INSTRUCTIONS FOR TEDDY'S SLIPOVER

BACK

★ Using 2 mm needles and A, cast on 67 sts.
Work 8 rows in rib as given for child's slipover, inc
1 st at end of last row: 68 sts. ★
Change to 3 mm needles.
Work in st st until back measures 9cm from beg,
ending with a P row.

□ = A   ●● = B

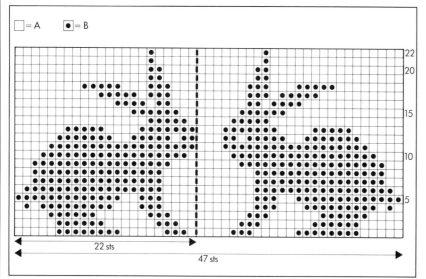

22 sts

47 sts

*"Run rabbit, run rabbit, run,
  run, run,
Here comes the farmer with
  his gun, gun, gun.
He'll get by without his rabbit
  pie,
So run rabbit, run rabbit,
  run."*

Shape armholes

Next row: K4 sts and slip these sts onto a safety-pin, K to end.

Next row: P4 sts and slip these sts onto a safety-pin, P to end: 60 sts.

Dec 1 st each end of next 4 rows: 52 sts.

Work straight until back measures 16·5 cm from beg, ending with a P row.

Shape neck

Next row: K10, K2 tog, turn and leave remaining sts on a spare needle.

Continue to dec 1 st at neck edge on every row until 8 sts remain. Now cast off.

Return to sts on spare needle.

With right side facing, slip first 28 sts onto a holder, rejoin yarn and complete to match first side of neck, reversing all shaping.

FRONT

Work as given for back from ★ to ★.

Change to 3 mm needles. Now work 2 rows st st. Place single rabbit motif as indicated in chart as follows:

Row 1: K24A, 3B, 5A, 8B, 28A.

Row 2: P28A, 6B, 6A, 3B, 25A.

Continue in this way, working from chart until row 22 has been completed.

Shape neck

Next row: K20, turn and leave remaining sts on a spare needle.

Dec 1 st at neck edge on every row until 8 sts remain. Work straight until front measures same as back to shoulders, ending P row.

Cast off.

Return to sts on spare needle.

With right side facing, slip first 12 sts onto a holder, rejoin yarn and complete to match first side of neck, reversing all shaping.

NECKBAND

Join left shoulder seam.

With right side facing and using 2 mm needles and A, pick up and K4 sts down right back neck, K across 28 sts from holder, pick up and K4 sts up left back neck and 33 sts down left front neck, K across 12 sts from holder, then pick up and K34 sts up right front neck: 115 sts.

Work 6 rows in rib as given for child's slipover.

Cast off.

ARMBANDS

Join right shoulder and neckband seam.

With right side facing and using 2 mm needles and A, pick up and K85 sts evenly round armhole including the 4 sts at each end on safety-pins.

Complete as given for neckband.

TO MAKE UP

Join side and armband seams. Press lightly following instructions on ball band.

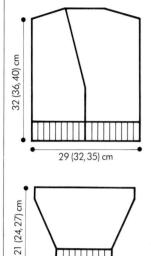

29 (32, 35) cm

32 (36, 40) cm

21 (24, 27) cm

EASTER CHICKS

A straightforward cardigan covered in Easter chicks.

MEASUREMENTS

To fit chest 46(51,56) cm [18(20,22) in]
Actual measurements 59(64,69) cm
Length to shoulders 32(36,40) cm
Sleeve seam 21(24,27) cm

MATERIALS

3(3,4) × 50 g balls of Patons Diploma 4 ply in main
colour A
1 ball same in contrast colour B
1 ball same in contrast colour C
3 buttons
A pair each of 2¾ mm (No 12) and 3¼ mm (No 10)
knitting needles and one 2¾ mm (No 12) circular
needle

TENSION

28 sts and 32 rows to 10cm measured over st st
worked on 3¼ mm needles

INSTRUCTIONS

BACK

Using 2¾ mm needles and A, cast on 82(90,98) sts.
Rib row 1: K2, ✳ P2, K2, rep from ✳ to end.
Rib row 2: P2, ✳ K2, P2, rep from ✳ to end.
Rep these 2 rows once more.
Change to B and work 2 rows rib, then change back
to A and continue in rib until work measures 5 cm,
ending rib row 2.
Change to 3¼ mm needles.

Proceed in st st, working in patt from chart and
repeating patt as necessary until work measures
32(36,40) cm from beg, ending with a P row.
Shape shoulders
Cast off 13(14,16) sts at beg of next 2 rows and
13(15,16) sts at beg of following 2 rows.
Cut off yarn and leave remaining 30(32,34) sts on a
holder.

LEFT FRONT

Using 2¾ mm needles and A, cast on 38(42,46) sts
and work in rib as given on back for 4 rows.
Change to B and work 2 rows rib, then change back
to A and continue in rib until work measures 5 cm.
Change to 3¼ m needles.
Proceed in st st, working in patt from chart as
indicated until work measures 14(16,18) cm, ending
with a K row.
Shape neck
Keeping patt correct, dec 1 st at beg of next and
every following 4th row until 26(29,32) sts remain.
Work straight until front measures same as back to
shoulder, ending at armhole edge.
Shape shoulder
Cast off 13(14,16) sts at beg of next row and
13(15,16) sts at beg of following alternate row.

RIGHT FRONT

Work as given for left front, reversing all shaping
and working from chart as indicated for right front.

SLEEVES

Using 2¾ mm needles and A, cast on 42(46,50) sts.
Work in rib as given on back for 4 rows.
Change to B and work 2 rows in rib. Change back to
A and continue in rib until work measures 5 cm.

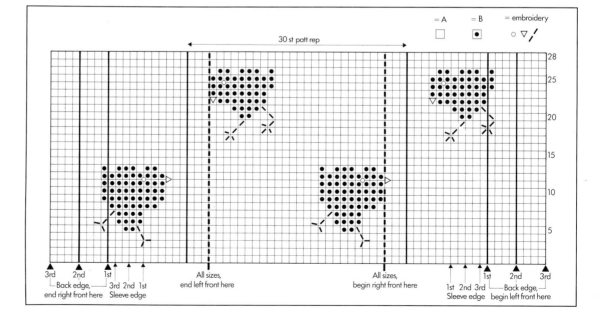

= A   = B   = embroidery

30 st patt rep

3rd 2nd 1st
Back edge,
end right front here

3rd 2nd 1st
Sleeve edge

All sizes,
end left front here

All sizes,
begin right front here

1st 2nd 3rd
Sleeve edge

Back edge,
begin left front here

1st 2nd 3rd

Spring-time wouldn't be the same without baby chicks and this classic V-neck cardigan is covered in them! They are knitted in as the cardigan is made – though they can be Swiss-darned on afterwards.

Change to 3¼ mm needles.
Proceed in st st, working in patt from chart as indicated for sleeve and AT THE SAME TIME inc and work into patt 1 st each end of 3rd and every following 3rd(4th,4th) row until there are 76(80,84) sts.
Work straight until sleeve measures 21(24,27) cm, ending with a P row.
Cast off.

BUTTON AND BUTTONHOLE BORDER
Join shoulder seams.
With right side facing and using the 2¾ mm circular needle, pick up and K44(51,56) sts up right front to beg of neck shaping and 56(64,72) sts up right front neck to shoulder seam, K across 30(32,34) sts from back neck holder, then pick up and K56(64,72) sts down left front neck to beg of neck shaping and 44(51,56) sts down left front to cast-on edge: 230(262, 290) sts.
Beg rib row 2, work 3 rows rib as given for back, ending with right side facing.
Buttonhole row: Rib 6, [cast off 3, rib 14(17,20) sts] twice, cast off 3, rib to end.
Next row: Rib to end, casting on 3 sts over those cast off.
Change to B and work 2 rows rib, then change back to A and work 2 rows rib.
Using A, cast off in rib.

TO MAKE UP
Using C, embroider beaks and feet on chicks.
Placing centre of tops of sleeves to shoulder seams, sew in sleeves. Join side and sleeve seams. Sew on buttons to correspond with buttonholes. Press lightly following instructions on ball band.

OH DUCKY!

This lightweight woollen pinafore has a little duck on its cross-over front.

MEASUREMENTS

To fit chest 46–51(51-56) cm [18–20(20–22) in]
Length to shoulders 43(48) cm

MATERIALS

3 × 50 g balls Woolgatherers 4 ply Superwash in main colour A
1 ball same in each of two contrast colours B and C
A pair each of 3 mm (No 11) and 3¼ mm (No 10) knitting needles

TENSION

28 sts and 38 rows to 10 cm measured over st st worked using 3¼ mm needles

INSTRUCTIONS

BACK

★ Using 3¼ mm needles and B, cast on 140(164) sts.
K 1 row.
Change to C and K 2 rows.
Change to B and K 2 rows.
Rep these 4 rows 4 times more.
Break off B and C.
Change to A.
Working in A only, continue in st st until work measures 24(27·5) cm from beg, ending with a K row.
Next row: (Wrong side) K1, P1, ★ P2 tog, rep from ★ to last 2 sts, P1, K1: 72(84) sts.
Waistband
Change to 3 mm needles.
Working in stripes of 2 rows B, 2 rows C, K 22 rows. ★
Using B, cast off.

FRONT

Work as given for back from ★ to ★, but do not cast off.
Left front bib
Next row: Using B, cast off 8(12) sts changing to A for the last st, change to 3¼ mm needles then K until there are 40(42) sts on the needle, turn and leave remaining 24(30) sts on a spare needle.
Break off B.
Next row: K5, P to last 5 sts, K5.
Next row: K.
Next row: K5, P to last 5 sts, K5.
Work motif from chart and shape bib as follows:
Next row: K12A, 6B, 15(17)A, with A K2 tog, K5.
Next row: K5A, P13(15)A, 11B, 5A, K5A.
Keeping 5 st g st border on each edge and decreasing 1 st at neck edge within border as before on next and every following alternate row, continue to work from chart until row 16 has been completed.
Now continue to dec at neck edge as before until 16(18) sts remain.
Continue without shaping until work measures 30·5(36) cm from top of waistband, ending wrong-side row.
Cast off.
Right front bib
With right side facing and using 3¼ mm needles and A, pick up and K the back loops of the last 24 sts from behind the left front bib, K across the first 16(18) sts from spare needle, then changing to a 3 mm needle and an odd length of B, cast off the final 8(12) sts.
Continuing on these 40(42) sts and using A, complete to match left front bib, omitting motif and working K2 tog tbl when decreasing.

TO MAKE UP

Join side seams of skirt. Sew ends of straps to waistband at back. Press lightly following instructions on ball band.

This 4 ply woollen pinafore is ideal for those bright spring days when, although it's tempting to throw off heavy winter woollies, it's not yet warm enough for cotton. The pinafore has bands of garter stitch at the hem and high waist, and a little duck motif on the cross-over front.

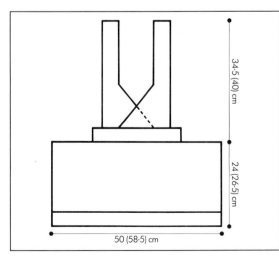

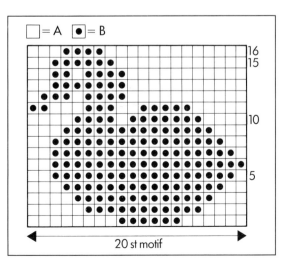

☐ = A   ● = B

20 st motif

SPRING CABLE

This little raglan sweater has an unusual cable design on its cuffs, waist and neck.

MEASUREMENTS

To fit chest 46–51(51–56) cm [18–20(20–22) in]
Actual measurements 61(66) cm
Length to shoulders 28(33) cm
Sleeve seam 20(23) cm

MATERIALS

4 × 50 g balls Woolgatherers 4 ply Superwash
A pair each of 3 mm (No 11) and 3¾ mm (No 9) knitting needles
Cable needle

TENSION

26 sts and 36 rows to 10 cm measured over patt worked on 3¾ mm needles

A thick, textured sweater in 4 ply yarn that is ideal for those breezy spring days when there is still a sharp chill in the air.

SPECIAL ABBREVIATIONS

C4, Cable 4 as follows: slip next 2 sts onto cable needle and hold at back of work, K2, then K2 from cable needle.
C3B, Cable 3 back as follows: slip next 2 sts onto cable needle and hold at back of work, K1, then K2 from cable needle.
C3F, Cable 3 front as follows: slip next st onto cable needle and hold at front of work, K2, then K1 from cable needle.
C6, Cable 6 as follows: slip next 3 sts onto cable needle and hold at back of work, K3, then K3 from cable needle.

INSTRUCTIONS

BACK

★ Using 3mm needles cast on 80(86) sts.
Beg welt patt as follows:
Row 1: K1, P1, ★ K4, P2, rep from ★ to last 6 sts, K4, P1, K1.
Row 2 and every alternate row: K2, ★ P4, K2, rep from ★ to end.
Row 3: K1, P1, ★ K4, P2, rep from ★ to last 6 sts, K4, P1, K1.
Row 5: K1, P1, ★ C4, P2, rep from ★ to last 6 sts, C4, P1, K1.
Rows 7 to 18: Rep rows 3 to 6 three times.
Row 19: P. ★
Row 20: Inc in first st, P to last st, K1: 81(87) sts.
Change to 3¾ mm needles.
Work in patt as follows:
Row 1: K.
Row 2: K1, P to last st, K1.
Row 3: K2, ★ P2, K1, rep from ★ to last st, K1.
Row 4: As row 2. These 4 rows form the patt.

Continue in patt until back measures 15(18) cm from beg, ending with a 4th patt row.
Shape raglan
Cast off 4 sts at beg of next 2 rows: 73(79) sts.
Work 4 rows straight in patt.
Next row: K1, K2 tog tbl, patt to last 3 sts, K2 tog, K1.
Work 3 rows straight.
Rep the last 4 rows until 67(73) sts remain, then dec on every alternate row until 57 sts remain, ending wrong-side row.
Divide for back opening
Next row: K1, K2 tog tbl, patt across 23 sts, K3, turn and leave remaining sts on a spare needle.
Next row K3, patt to end.
Continuing to work 3 sts in g st at neck edge, dec 1 st as before at raglan edge on next and every following alternate row until 22 sts remain.
Next row: (Buttonhole row) K1, K2 tog tbl, patt 16, yrn, K2 tog, K1.
Next row: K3, patt to end.
Now continue decreasing as before until 17 sts remain.
Break off yarn and leave sts on a holder.
Return to remaining sts.
With right side facing, join yarn to first st and cast on 4 sts, patt to last 3 sts, K2 tog, K1: 32 sts.
Next row: Patt to last 4 sts, K4.
Continuing to work 4 sts in g st at neck edge, dec 1 st as before at raglan edge on next and every following alternate row until 20 sts remain.
Break off yarn and leave sts on holder.

FRONT

Work as given for back from ★ to ★.
Next row: K1, P to last st, K1: 80(86) sts.
Change to 3¾ mm needles.
Work in patt with central cable panel as follows:
Row 1: K26(29), P2, K7, P2, K6, P2, K7, P2, K26(29).
Row 2: K1, P25(28), K2, P7, K2, P6, K2, P7, K2, P25(28), K1.
Row 3: K2, [P2, K1] 8(9) times, P2, C3B, K1, C3F, P2, C6, P2, C3B, K1, C3F, P2, [K1, P2] 8(9) times, K2.
Row 4: As row 2.
These 4 rows form patt.
Continue in patt until front measures same as back to beg of raglan shaping, ending with a 4th patt row.
Shape raglan
Cast off 4 sts at beg of next 2 rows: 72(78) sts.
Work 4 rows straight in patt.
Next row: K1, K2 tog tbl, patt to last 3 sts, K2 tog, K1.
Work 3 rows straight.
Rep the last 4 rows until 66(72) sts remain, then dec on every alternate row until 52 sts remain, ending with a wrong-side row.
Divide for neck
Next row: K1, K2 tog tbl, patt 13, K2 tog, turn and leave remaining sts on a spare needle.
Continuing to dec at raglan edge as before, dec 1 st

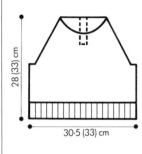

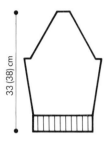

at neck edge on every row until 9 sts remain.
Keeping neck edge straight, continue to dec at
raglan edge only until 2 sts remain, ending with a
wrong-side row.
Cast off.
Return to remaining sts.
With right side facing, slip first 16 sts onto a holder,
join yarn to next st, K2 tog, patt to last 3 sts, K2 tog,
K1.
Now complete 2nd side of neck to match first side,
reversing all shaping.

SLEEVES

Using 3 mm needles cast on 44 sts.
Work rows 1 to 19 as given for welt patt on back.
Next row: Inc. in first st, P to last st, K1: 45 sts.
Change to 3¾ mm needles.
Working in patt as given for back, inc and work into
patt 1 st each end of 7th and every following 6th row
until there are 57(63) sts.
Work straight until sleeve measures 20(23) cm from
beg, ending with a 4th patt row.
Shape raglan
Cast off 4 sts at beg of next 2 rows: 49(55) sts.
Work 4 rows straight in patt.
Next row: K1, K2 tog tbl, patt to last 3 sts, K2 tog, K1.
Work 3 rows straight.
Rep the last 4 rows until 43(49) sts remain, then dec
on every alternate row until 9 sts remain, ending
wrong-side row.
Break off yarn and leave remaining sts on a holder.

NECKBAND

With right side facing and using 3mm needles, K20
sts from left back neck holder and 9 sts from top of
one sleeve, pick up and K20 sts down left side of
front neck, K across 16 sts from front neck holder,
pick up and K20 sts up right side of front neck, then K
across 9 sts from second sleeve and 17 sts from right
back neck holder: 111 sts.
Next row: P.
Now continue in patt as follows:
Row 1: K4, ✳ P2, K4, rep from ✳ to last 5 sts, P2, K3.
Row 2: K5, ✳ P4, K2, rep from ✳ to last 4 sts, K4.
Row 3: K4, ✳ P2, C4, rep from ✳ to last 5 sts, P2, yrn,
K2 tog, K1.
Row 4: As row 2.
Row 5: As row 1.
Row 6: As row 2.
Row 7: As row 3 to last 5 sts, then P2, K3.
Row 8: As row 2.
Cast off.

TO MAKE UP

Join raglan seams.
Sew lower edge of button border in place behind
buttonhole border. Sew on buttons.
Join side and sleeve seams.

LAURIE LAMBKIN

An adorable woolly lamb, just like the real thing!

MEASUREMENT

Height approximately 33 cm [13 in]

MATERIALS

150 g Bouclé yarn
Small amounts of plain 4 ply yarn for ear linings and
a little black and blue for embroidering the eyes
Polyester Filling
A pair each of 3¼ mm (No 10) and 4 mm (No 8)
knitting needles

TENSION

18 sts and 32 rows to 10 cm measured over g st

NOTE

The legs, body, head and ears are all worked in
garter st using bouclé yarn.

INSTRUCTIONS

LEFT FRONT LEG

✳✳ Using 4 mm needles and bouclé yarn, cast on
10 sts.
K 34 rows.
Next row: Inc in first st, K to end.
Next row: K to last st, inc in last st.
Rep these 2 rows until there are 18 sts.
Break off yarn and leave sts on a spare needle.

LEFT BACK LEG

Using 4 mm needles and bouclé yarn, cast on 10 sts.
K 24 rows.
Shape leg
Row 1: K to last st, inc in last st: 11 sts.
Row 2: K.
Rows 3 and 4: As rows 1 and 2: 12 sts.
Row 5: K2 tog, K to last st, inc in last st: 12 sts.
Row 6: K.
Rep rows 5 and 6 seven times more.
Join legs
K across 12 sts of back leg then K across 18 sts of
front leg: 30 sts. ✳
K 19 rows.
Shape back
Row 1: K2 tog, K to end.
Row 2: K to last 2 sts, K2 tog.
Rep these 2 rows until 24 sts remain.
Head
Row 1: Cast off 14 sts, K to last st, inc in last st: 11 sts.
Row 2: Inc in first st, K to last st, inc in last st: 13 sts.
Rows 3 to 7: Rep row 2 five times: 23 sts.
Row 8: K.
Row 9: [K5, inc in next st] 3 times, K5: 26 sts.

Soft bouclé yarn gives Laurie Lambkin a wonderfully warm fluffy fleece that really is just like the real thing. He's so sweet – even grown ups can't resist giving him a cuddle!

Rows 10 to 12: K.
Row 13: K to last 2 sts, K2 tog: 25 sts.
Row 14: K.
Rows 15 to 20: Rep rows 13 and 14 three times: 22 sts.
Dec 1 st each end of next and following alternate row: 18 sts.
Dec 1 st each end of every row until 8 sts remain.
Next row: K1, [sl 1, K1, psso] 3 times, K1: 5 sts.
Cast off. ★★

RIGHT FRONT, BACK LEGS, BODY AND HEAD
Work as given for left side from ★★ to ★★.

INSIDE LEG GUSSET (make 2)
Work as given for left front and back legs from ★★ to ★.
K 9 rows. Cast off.

EARS (make 2)
Using 4mm needles and bouclé yarn cast on 12 sts.
K 22 rows.
Shape top
Dec 1 st each end of next and every following alternate row until 4 sts remain.
K 1 row.

Next row: [K2 tog] twice: 2 sts. Now K 1 row.
Change to 3¼ mm needles and 4 ply yarn and work ear lining as follows:
Row 1: Inc into each st: 4 sts.
Row 2: P.
Row 3: Inc into each st: 8 sts.
Row 4: P.
Continuing in st st, inc 1 st each end of next and every following alternate row until there are 20 sts.
Work straight until lining measures the same length as outer ear, ending with a wrong-side row. Cast off.

TAIL
Using 4 mm needles and bouclé yarn, cast on 28 sts.
Work 8 rows rev st st. Cast off.

TO MAKE UP
Join side seams on ears. Join leg gussets to legs and body, joining seam at top of gusset. Join seam around head and down centre back leaving a small opening at back of head for filling. Turn out to right side and fill firmly, then close opening neatly. Fold ears in half at base and stitch into place at sides of head. Embroider eyes and nose as shown in picture. Join seam on tail and sew into place.

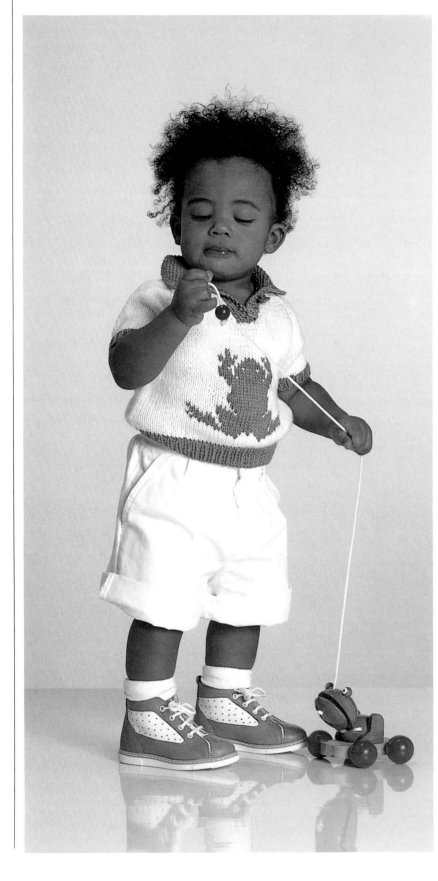

FREDDY FROG

A cotton top with a handsome frog motif.

MEASUREMENTS

To fit chest 46(51,56) cm [18(20,22) in]
Actual measurements 53(59,64) cm
Length to shoulders 28(30·5,33) cm
Sleeve seam 6(8,10) cm

MATERIALS

3(4,4) × 50 g balls of Phildar Satine No 4 in main colour A
1(2,2) balls of same in contrast colour B
A pair each of 3¼ mm (No 10) and 4 mm (No 8) knitting needles
2 buttons

TENSION

22 sts and 28 rows to 10 cm measured over st st

INSTRUCTIONS

BACK

✷ Using 3¼ mm needles and B, cast on 55(61,67) sts.
Rib row 1: K2, ✷ Pl, K1, rep from ✷ to last st, K1.
Rib row 2: K1, ✷ P1, K1, rep from ✷ to end.
Rep these 2 rows 4 times more.
Change to 4 mm needles.
Break off B. Join in A.
Inc row: K10(14,16), ✷ inc in next st, K10, rep from ✷ to last 12(14,18) sts, inc in next st, K to end:
59(65,71) sts. ✷
Beg P row, work in st st until back measures 15(16·5,19) cm from beg, ending P row.
Shape raglans
Cast off 3(3,4) sts at beg of next 2 rows:
53(59,63) sts.
Work 2 rows st st.
Next row: K1, K2 tog tbl, K to last 3 sts, K2 tog, K1.
Next row: P.
Rep these 2 rows until 21(23,27) sts remain, ending P row.
Break off yarn and leave remaining sts on a holder.

SLEEVES

Using 3¼ mm needles and B, cast on 41(45,47)sts.
Work 6 rows in rib as given for back.
Change to 4 mm needles.
Break off B. Join A.
Inc row: K8(9,10), ✷ inc in next st, K7(8,9), rep from ✷ to last 9(9,10)sts, inc in next st, K to end:
45(49,51)sts.
Beg P row, work in st st until sleeve measures 6(8,10) cm from beg, ending with a P row.
Shape raglan
Cast off 3(3,4)sts at beg of next 2 rows: 39(43,43)sts.

Work 2 rows st st.
Next row: K1, K2 tog tbl, K to last 3 sts, K2 tog, K1.
Next row: P.
Rep these 2 rows until 7 sts remain, ending with a P row.
Break off yarn.
Leave sts on a holder.

FRONT

Work as given for back from ★ to ★.
Beg P row, work 3 rows st st.
Now work frog motif from chart as follows:
Row 1: K26(29,32)A, 1B, 5A, 1B, 26(29,32)A.
Row 2: P24(27,30)A, 3B, 5A, 3B, 24(27,30)A.
Continue in patt from chart until row 30 has been completed.
Continue in A only until front measures same as back to beg of raglan shaping, ending P row.
Shape raglans
Work raglan shaping as given for back until 49(55,59) sts remain, ending with a P row.
Divide for neck
Next row: K1, K2 tog tbl, K19(22,24), turn and leave remaining sts on a spare needle.
Next row: Join on B and cast on 5 sts for button band, over these 5 sts work [K1, P1] twice, K1, change to A and P to end.
★★ Always twisting A and B together when changing colour to avoid making a hole, keep 5 st border worked in moss st and B as set and AT THE SAME TIME continue raglan shaping as before in A until 17(20,22) sts remain, ending with a wrong-side row.★★
Shape neck
Next row: K1, K2 tog tbl, K4(6,6), K2 tog, K1, turn and leave remaining sts on a safety-pin.
Next row: P1, P2 tog, P to end.
Next row: K1, K2 tog tbl, K to last 3 sts, K2 tog, K1.
Next row: P1, P2 tog, P to end: 4(5,5) sts.
Now continue to dec at raglan edge only as before until 2 sts remain.
Cast off.
Return to sts on spare needle.
With right side facing, join B to first st and K5, join in A then K to last 3 sts, K2 tog, K1.
Continuing to dec at raglan edge on every alternate row as before and working 5 st border in moss st and B, work as given for first side of neck from ★★ to ★★, working buttonhole on the 7th row as follows:
Buttonhole row: (Right side) K1, P1, yrn, sl 1, K1, psso, K1, change to A and K to last 3 sts, K2 tog, K1.
Shape neck
Do not cut off B. Slip first 7(8,10) sts onto a safety-pin, using A only K1, K2 tog tbl, K to last 3 sts, K2 tog, K1.
Dec 1 st at neck edge on next 2 rows and AT THE SAME TIME continue to dec at raglan edge as before until 2 sts remain.
Cast off.

COLLAR

With right side facing and using 3¼ mm needles and yarn from right front border at neck edge, work across sts on safety-pin as follows: K1, P1, yrn, sl 1, K1, psso, K3(4,6), pick up and K9(11,11) sts up right side of front neck, K across 7 sts from top of right sleeve, 21(23,27) sts across back neck and 7 sts across top of left sleeve, pick up and K9(11,11) sts down left side of front neck, K the first 3(4,6) sts from safety-pin, then [P1, K1] twice: 67(75, 83) sts.
Work 2 rows in moss st. Continuing in moss st, cast off 2 sts at beg of next 2 rows.
Work a further 16 rows moss st.
Cast off.

TO MAKE UP

Join raglan seams, then join side and sleeve seams. Catch button border in place at base of buttonhole border. Sew on buttons. Press lightly following instructions on ball band.

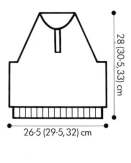

A practical short-sleeved raglan top, ideal for mischievous rascals of the 'slugs and snails and puppy dogs' tails variety!

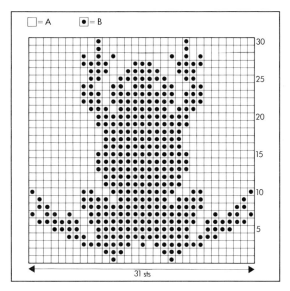

☐ = A   ● = B
31 sts

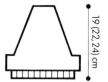

28 (30·5, 33) cm
26·5 (29·5, 32) cm
19 (22, 24) cm

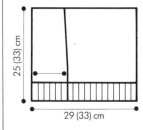

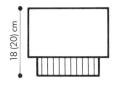

25 (33) cm

29 (33) cm

18 (20) cm

SUGAR AND SPICE

A traditional twinset in a delicate lacy stitch, with an unusual low front fastening.

MEASUREMENTS
To fit chest 56(61) cm [22(24) in]
Actual measurements: 58(66) cm
Cardigan
Length to shoulders 25(33) cm
Sweater
Length to shoulders 23(30) cm

MATERIALS
Cardigan
1(2) × 40 g balls Sirdar Snuggly 2 ply
4 buttons
Sweater
1(2) × 40 g balls Sirdar Snuggly 2 ply
2 buttons
A pair each of 2¾ mm (No 12) and 3¼ mm (No 10) knitting needles
2·00 mm crochet hook

TENSION
2 pattern repeats (20 sts) and 25 rows measure 6 cm over pattern using 3¼ mm needles.

INSTRUCTIONS FOR CARDIGAN

BACK
Using 2¾ mm needles cast on 93(103) sts.
Rib row 1: S1 1, K1, * P1, K1, rep.from * to last st, K1.
Rib row 2: S1 1, * P1, K1, rep from * to end.
Rep these 2 rows 10 times more.
Change to 3¼ mm needles.
Proceed in patt as follows:
Row 1: S1 1, K1, * yf, skpo, K2 tog, yf, K1, rep from * to last st, K1.
Row 2 and every alternate row: S1 1, P to last st, K1.
Row 3: S1 1, K2, * yf, skpo, K3, K2 tog, yf, K3, rep from * to end.
Row 5: S1 1, K3 * yf, skpo, K1, K2 tog, yf, K5, rep from * to last 9 sts, yf, skpo, K1, K2 tog, yf, K4.
Row 7: S1 1, K4 * yf, s1 1, K2 tog, psso, yf, K7, rep from * to last 8 sts, yf, s1 1, K2 tog, psso, yf, K5.
Row 9: S1 1, K1, * skpo, K2, yf, K1, yf, K2, K2 tog, K1, rep from * to last st, K1.
Row 11: As row 9.
Row 13: As row 9.
Row 14: S1 1, P to last st, K1.
These 14 rows form the patt.
Continue in patt until work measures 25(33) cm from beg, ending with a wrong-side row.
Shape shoulders
Cast off 30(34) sts in patt at beg of next 2 rows.
Cast off remaining 33 sts in patt.

LEFT FRONT
* Using 2¾ mm needles cast on 33(43) sts.
Work 22 rows in rib as given for back. *
Change to 3¼ mm needles.
Work rows 1 to 14 of patt as given for back.
Shape front edge
Keeping patt correct, dec 1 st at end of next and every following 24th(40th) row until 30(34) sts remain.
Work straight until front measures same as back, ending with a wrong-side row. Cast off in patt.

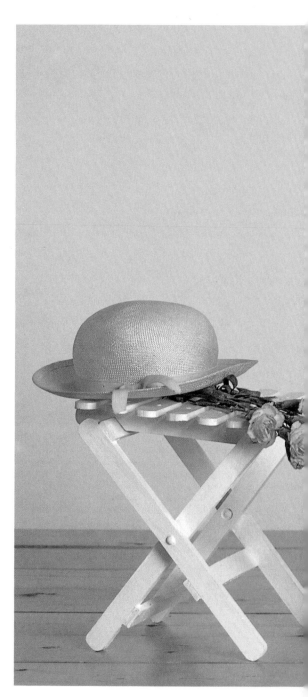

"What are little girls made of?
What are little girls made of?
Sugar and spice and all things nice,
That's what little girls are made of."

RIGHT FRONT

Work as given for left front from ★ to ★.
Change to 3¼ mm needles.
Work rows 1 to 14 of patt as given for back.

Shape front edge

Keeping patt correct, dec 1 st at beg of next and every following 24th(40th) row until 30(34) sts remain.
Work straight until front measures same as back, ending with a right-side row.
Cast off purlwise.

SLEEVES

Using 2¾ mm needles cast on 51(55) sts.
Rib row 1: Sl 1, K1, ★ P1, K1, rep from ★ to last st, K1.
Rib row 2: Sl 1, ★ P1, K1, rep from ★ to end.
Rep these 2 rows 9 times more, then rib row 1 again.
Inc row: Sl 1, rib 1(3), ★ inc in next st, P1, rep from ★ to last 3 sts, rib to end: 73(83) sts.
Change to 3¼ mm needles.
Work in patt as given for back until sleeve measures 18(20) cm from beg, ending with a wrong-side row.
Cast off in patt.

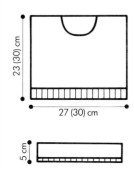

23 (30) cm

27 (30) cm

5 cm

RIGHT FRONT BORDER

Join shoulder seams.
Using 2¾ mm needles cast on 35 sts.
Row 1: S1 1, K1, * P1, K1, rep from * to last st, K1.
Row 2: S1 1, * P1, K1, rep from * to end.
Rep these 2 rows once more.
Row 5: S1 1, [K1, P1] twice, K1, cast off 2 sts, [K1, P1] 9 times, cast off 2 sts, [P1, K1] twice, K1.
Row 6: S1 1, [P1, K1] twice, P1, cast on 2 sts, [K1, P1] 9 times, K1, cast on 2 sts, [P1, K1] 3 times.
Rows 7 to 16: Rep rows 1 and 2 five times.
Rows 17 and 18: Rep rows 5 and 6 once.
Rows 19 to 22: Rep rows 1 and 2 twice.
Row 23: Cast off 20 sts in rib, [K1, P1] 6 times, K2: 15 sts.
Row 24: S1 1, * P1, K1, rep from * to end.
Continue in rib, dec 1 st at end of the 43rd row from beg and every following 16th row until 11 sts remain.
Work straight until border is long enough to go up front and round to centre back neck, ending with a wrong-side row.
Cast off in rib.

LEFT FRONT BORDER

Using 2¾ mm needles cast on 35 sts.
Row 1: S1 1, K1, * P1, K1, rep from * to last st, K1.
Row 2: S1 1, * P1, K1, rep from * to end.
Rep these 2 rows 10 times more.
Row 23: S1 1, [K1, P1] 7 times, cast off remaining 20 sts in rib, then fasten off.
Row 24: With wrong side facing, rejoin yarn to remaining 15 sts, K1, [P1, K1] 7 times.
Continue in rib, dec 1 st at beg of the 43rd row from beg and every following 16th row until 11 sts remain.
Work straight until border is long enough to go up front and round to centre back neck, ending with a wrong-side row.
Cast off in rib.

TO MAKE UP

Placing centre of tops of sleeves to shoulder seams, sew in sleeves.
Join side and sleeve seams.
Join ends of borders, then placing seam to centre back neck, sew front borders in position. Sew on buttons to correspond with buttonholes. Press lightly following instructions on ball band.

INSTRUCTIONS FOR SWEATER

BACK

★★ Using 2¾ mm needles cast on 89(99) sts.
Rib row 1: S1 1, K1, * P1, K1, rep from * to last st, K1.
Rib row 2: S1 1, * P1, K1, rep from * to end.
Rep these 2 rows 6 times more.
Change to 3¼ mm needles.
Proceed in patt as follows:
Row 1: S1 1, K1, K2 tog, yf, K1, * yf, skpo, K2 tog, yf, K1, rep from * to last 4 sts, yf, skpo, K2.
Row 2 and every alternate row: S1 1, P to last st, K1.
Row 3: S1 1, * yf, skpo, K3, K2 tog, yf, K3, rep from * to last 8 sts, yf, skpo, K3, K2 tog, yf, K1.
Row 5: S1 1, K1, * yf, skpo, K1, K2 tog, yf, K5, rep from * to last 7 sts, yf, skpo, K1, K2 tog, yf, K2.
Row 7: S1 1, K2, * yf, s1 1, K2 tog, psso, yf, K7, rep from * to last 6 sts, yf, s1 1, K2 tog, psso, yf, K3.
Row 9: S1 1, K4, yf, K2, K2 tog, K1, * skpo, K2, yf, K1, yf, K2, K2 tog, K1, rep from * to last 9 sts, skpo, K2, yf, K5.
Row 11: As row 9.
Row 13: As row 9.
Row 14: S1 1, P to last st, K1.
These 14 rows form the patt. ★★
Continue in patt until work measures 15(23) cm from beg, ending with a wrong-side row.
Divide for back opening
Next row: S1 1, patt 43(48) sts, K2 tog, patt 42(47) sts, K1.
Next row: S1 1, patt 42(47), K1, turn and leave remaining sts on a spare needle.
Work straight until back measures 23(30) cm from beg, ending with a right-side row.
Shape shoulder
Next row: Cast off 28(33) sts purlwise, P to last st, K1.
Break off yarn and leave remaining 16 sts on a holder.
With wrong side facing, rejoin yarn to remaining sts and proceed as follows:
Next row: S1 1, patt to last st, K1.
Work straight until back measures 23(30) cm from beg, ending with a wrong-side row.
Shape shoulder
Next row: Cast off 28(33) sts in patt, patt to last st, K1.
Next row: S1 1, P to last st, K1.
Break off yarn and leave remaining 16 sts on a holder.

FRONT

Work as given for back from ★★ to ★★.
Continue in patt until work measures 18(25) cm from beg, ending with a wrong-side row.

Shape neck

Next row: Sl 1, patt 35(40) sts, turn and leave remaining sts on a spare needle.
Next row: Sl 1, P to last st, K1.
Dec 1 st at neck edge on next 8 rows: 28(33) sts.
Work straight until front measures same as back, ending with a wrong-side row.
Cast off in patt.
Return to remaining sts.
With right side facing, slip first 17 sts onto a holder, and rejoin yarn to remaining sts.
Proceed as follows:
Next row: K1, patt to last st, K1.
Next row: Sl 1, P to last st, K1.
Dec 1 st at neck edge on next 8 rows: 28(33) sts.
Work straight until front measures same as back, ending with a right-side row.
Cast off purlwise.

SLEEVES

Using 2¾ mm needles cast on 79 sts.
Rib row 1: Sl 1, K1, ★ P1, K1, rep from ★ to last st, K1.
Rib row 2: Sl 1, ★ P1, K1, rep from ★ to end.
Rep these 2 rows twice more.
Change to 3¼ mm needles.
Work rows 1 to 14 as given for back.
Cast off in patt.

NECKBAND

Join shoulder seams.
With right side facing, using 2¾ mm needles and beg at left side of back neck, K across 16 sts on holder at back neck, pick up and K15 sts evenly down left side of front neck, K across 17 sts on front neck holder, pick up and K15 sts evenly up right side of front neck, then K across 16 sts from holder at right side of back neck: 79 sts.
Rib row 1: Sl 1, ★ P1, K1, rep from ★ to end.
Rib row 2: Sl 1, K1, ★ P1, K1, rep from ★ to last st, K1.
Rep these 2 rows twice more.
Now work rib row 1 again.
Cast off in rib.

BUTTONHOLE BORDER

With right side facing, using a 2.00 mm crochet hook and beg at top of right back opening, work 24 dc evenly down back opening, turn.
Row 1: 1 ch (to count as first dc), 1 dc into each of next 8 dc, 2 ch, miss 2 dc, 1 dc into each of next 8 dc, 2 ch, miss 2 dc, 1 dc into each of next 3 dc, turn.
Row 2: 1 ch, 1 dc into each of next 2 dc, 2 dc into 2 ch sp, 1 dc into each of next 8 dc, 2 dc into 2 ch sp, 1 dc into each of next 9 dc.
Fasten off.

BUTTON BORDER

With right side facing, using a 2.00 mm crochet hook and beg at lower edge of left back opening, work 24 dc evenly up back opening, turn.
Work 2 rows in dc.
Fasten off.

TO MAKE UP

Placing centre of tops of sleeves to shoulder seams, sew in sleeves. Join side and sleeve seams. Overlap buttonhole border over button border and stitch into position at lower edge. Sew on buttons to correspond with buttonholes. Press lightly following instructions on ball band.

The appeal of a traditional twinset is as timeless as the popularity of delicate lacy stitches like this one, which makes this twinset ideal for mild spring weather. See stitch detail opposite.

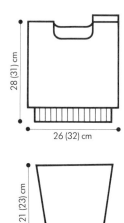

28 (31) cm

26 (32) cm

21 (23) cm

BASKET WEAVE

A round-neck jumper with shoulder fastening. The interesting woven effect is created by interweaving three different stitches.

MEASUREMENTS

To fit chest 46–51(51–56) cm [18–20(20–22) in]
Actual measurements 52(64) cm
Length to shoulders 28(31) cm
Sleeve seam 21(23) cm

MATERIALS

3(4) × 50 g balls King Cole Superwash 4 ply
A pair each of 2¼ mm (No 13) and 3 mm (No 11) knitting needles
4 buttons

TENSION

36 sts and 48 rows to 10 cm measured over patt

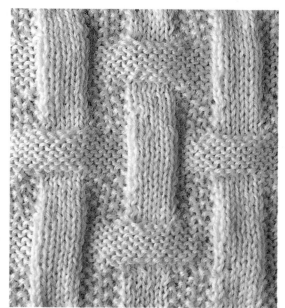

INSTRUCTIONS

BACK

With 2¼mm needles cast on 94(114)sts.
Rib row 1: K2, ✳ P2, K2, rep from ✳ to end.
Rib row 2: K1, P1, ✳ K2, P2, rep from ✳ to last 4 sts, K2, Pl, K1.
Rep these 2 rows for 4cm, ending rib row 1.
Inc row: Rib 16(24), ✳ inc in next st, rib 15, rep from ✳ to last 14(26)sts, inc in next st, rib to end: 99(119) sts.
Change to 3 mm needles.
Proceed in patt as follows:
Row 1: K2, ✳ [K1, P1] twice, K6, rep from ✳ to last 7 sts, [K1, P1] twice, K3.

Row 2: K1, P1, ✳ [K1, P1] twice, K1, P5, rep from ✳ to last 7 sts, [K1, P1] twice, K1, P1, K1.
Rows 3 to 8: Rep rows 1 and 2 three times.
Row 9: K2, P15(5), ✳ K5, P15, rep from ✳ to last 22(12) sts, K5, P15(5), K2.
Row 10: K1, P1, K15(5), ✳ P5, K15, rep from ✳ to last 22(12) sts, P5, K15(5), P1, K1.
Rows 11 to 14: Rep rows 9 and 10 twice.
Rows 15 to 22: Rep rows 1 and 2 four times.
Row 23: K2, P5(15), ✳ K5, P15, rep from ✳ to last 12(22) sts, K5, P5(15), K2.
Row 24: K1, P1, K5(15), ✳ P5, K15, rep from ✳ to last 12(22) sts, P5, K5(15), P1, K1.
Rows 25 to 28: Rep rows 23 and 24 twice.
These 28 rows form the patt.
Continue in patt until back measures approximately 26(29) cm from beg, ending with row 18(4).
Shape neck
Next row: Patt across 35(41) sts, turn and leave remaining sts on spare needle.
Keeping patt correct, dec 1 st at neck edge on every row until 27(33) sts remain.
Cast off.
Return to sts on spare needle.
With right side facing, slip first 29(37) sts onto a holder, rejoin yarn to next st and using 2¼ mm needles, work in moss st to end of row.
Continuing in moss st, dec 1 st at neck edge on every row until 27(33) sts remain.
Cast off.

FRONT

Work as given for back until 22 rows less than back to shoulders have been worked, ending with row 6(20).
Shape neck
Next row: Patt across 39(45) sts, turn and leave remaining sts on a spare needle.
Keeping patt correct, dec 1 st at neck edge on every row until 27(33) sts remain.
Work straight until front measures same as back to shoulders.
Change to 2¼ mm needles and work buttonhole border as follows:
Work 4 rows moss st.
Next row: (Buttonhole row) Moss st 7(9), ★ yrn, sl 1, K1, psso, moss st 6(8), rep from ★ once more, yrn, sl 1, K1, psso, moss st 2.
Work 3 rows moss st.
Cast off.
Return to sts on spare needle.
With right side facing, slip first 21(29) sts onto a holder, rejoin yarn and patt to end.
Keeping patt correct, dec 1 st at neck edge on every row until 27(33) sts remain.
Work straight until front measures same as back to right shoulder, ending wrong-side row.
Cast off.

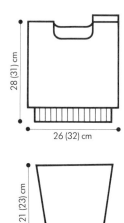

This clever basket weave effect is created by combining stocking stitch, reversed stocking stitch and moss stitch. The result is a warm sweater with quite a lot of stretch in it!

SLEEVES

Using 2¼ mm needles cast on 46(54) sts.
Work 4 cm in rib as given for back, ending rib row 1.
Inc row: Rib 4(2), ★ inc in next st, rib 2(11), rep from ★
to last 5(3) sts, inc in next st, rib 4(2): 59 sts.
Change to 3 mm needles.
Now working in patt as given for first size of back,
inc and work into patt 1 st within the 2 st border at
each end of 5th and every following 4th row until
there are 79(89) sts.
Work straight until sleeve measures approximately
21(23) cm from beg, ending with row 28(8).
Cast off.

NECKBAND

With right side facing and using 2¼ mm needles,
pick up and K26 sts down left side of front neck, K
across 21(29) sts on front neck holder, pick up and
K18 sts up right side of front neck and 8 sts down
right side of back neck, K across 29(37) sts on back
neck holder, then pick up and K8 sts up left side of
back neck: 110(126) sts. Now P 1 row.
Work 5 rows in rib as given for back.
Buttonhole row: Rib to last 5 sts, P2 tog, yrn, rib to
end.
Work 5 more rows in rib.
Cast off.

TO MAKE UP

Overlap buttonhole border on left shoulder and
catch together at armhole edge.
Sew in sleeves, then join side and sleeve seams.
Sew on buttons.

EGG COSIES

Three Easter egg cosies.

MATERIALS

Oddments of 4 ply yarn
For the Rabbit
Grey main, white contrast
For the Mouse
Pink main, white contrast
For the Chicken
White main, red contrast
Also a small length of black for embroidery on the
Rabbit and Mouse
A pair each of 3 mm (No 11), 3¼ mm (No 10) and
3¾ mm (No 9) knitting needles

INSTRUCTIONS

BASIC COSY

Using 3¾ mm needles and 2 strands of main colour
yarn together, cast on 39 sts.
Rib row 1: K1, ★ P1, K1, rep from ★ to end.
Rib row 2: P1, ★ K1, P1, rep from ★ to end.
Rep these 2 rows twice more, inc 1 st at end of last
row: 40 sts.
Beg K row, work 10 rows st st.
Shape Top
Row 1: ★ K5, K2 tog, rep from ★ to last 5 sts, K5: 35 sts.
Row 2 and every alternate row: P.
Row 3: ★ K4, K2 tog, rep from ★ to last 5 sts., K5: 30 sts.
Row 5: ★ K3, K2 tog, rep from ★ to end: 24 sts.
Row 7: K2, K2 tog, rep from ★ to end: 18 sts.
Row 8: P.
For Rabbit and Mouse: Break off yarn and thread
through sts, draw up tightly, then fasten off securely
and join back seem.
For Chicken: Divide the sts onto 2 needles with both
points facing the same way, then slip 1 st from each
needle onto a 3rd needle, pass the first of these 2 sts
on the 3rd needle over the 2nd and off the needle,
continue in this way to end of row: 9 sts. Break off
yarn. Join back seam.

RABBIT'S EARS (make 2)

Using 3¼ mm needles and 1 strand of main colour
yarn, cast on 12 sts
Beg K row, work 20 rows st st.
Dec 1 st each end of next and every following
alternate row until 4 sts remain.
Change to 3 mm needles and contrast colour for ear
linings.
Inc 1 st each end of next and every alternate row
until there are 12 sts.
Work 20 rows straight. Now cast off.
Join seams at sides of ears, fold ear at base and
stitch into place on cosy.

Easter eggs need Easter egg cosies. These are all created from the same basic cosy pattern. Use oddments of wool for them.

TO FINISH RABBIT

Using contrast colour, make a pompon by winding yarn round two fingers about 40 times, secure tightly round centre, then cut loops and fluff up. Sew pompon into position, then embroider rabbit's features as shown in picture.

MOUSE'S EARS (make 2)

Using 3¼ mm needles and 1 strand of main colour yarn, cast on 6 sts.
Working in st st, inc 1 st each end of first and every following alternate row until there are 12 sts.
Work 7 rows straight.
Dec 1 st each end of next 3 rows, work 1 row straight.
Change to 3mm needles and contrast colour for ear linings.
Work 1 row.
Inc. 1 st each end of next 3 rows: 12 sts.
Work 6 rows straight, then dec 1 st each end of next and every following alternate row until 6 sts remain.
Work 1 row and cast off.
Join seams at sides of ears, then gathering ear slightly at base, stitch into place on cosy.

MOUSE'S TAIL

Using 3¼ mm needles and 2 strands of main colour, cast on 26 sts, then cast off again. Sew into place.

TO FINISH MOUSE

Embroider features as shown in picture.

CHICKEN'S CREST

Using 3¼ mm needles and 1 strand of contrast colour and working across 9 sts on needle, K into front and back of each st to last st, K1: 17 sts.
Next row: P.
Working in st st, inc 1 st each end of next and following 2 alternate rows: 23 sts.
Next row: K1, ＊ yrn, sl 1, K1, psso, rep from ＊ to end.
Dec 1 st each end of next and every following alternate row until 17 sts remain. Now cast off.
Fold crest along row of holes and sew down cast off edge and join side seams.

CHICKEN'S BEAK

Using 3¼ mm needles and 1 strand of contrast colour, cast on 10 sts.
Working in st st, dec 1 st each end of 3rd and every following alternate row until 4 sts remain.
Next row: P2 tog twice.
Break off yarn and thread through sts.
Fold beak in half and join seam, then sew into place on cosy.

TO FINISH CHICKEN

Using contrast colour, embroider eyes as in picture.

CIRCUS TIME

Bring on the clowns... and the marching elephants, and the seals, and the balloons! This chapter contains a host of colourful and exciting designs to knit for babies, toddlers and, of course, Teddy. All are inspired by the circus ring, including Pierrot jumpers, an abstract cardigan and a knitted snake. With these and more, the following pages are full of surprises.

BIG TOP

A smart bomber jacket-style cardigan in a brilliantly coloured abstract design knitted in warm double knitting.

MEASUREMENTS
To fit chest 56(61,64)cm [22(24,25)in]
Actual measurements 64(68,72)cm
Length to shoulders 32(35,38)cm
Sleeve seam 26(28,32)cm

MATERIALS
2(2,3) × 50g balls Rowan Designer D.K. in main colour A
2 balls same in each of contrast colours B and C
1 ball same in each of contrast colours D and E
A pair each of 3¼mm (No 10) and 4mm (No 8) knitting needles
6 buttons

TENSION
24 sts and 28 rows to 10cm measured over st st worked on 4mm needles

INSTRUCTIONS

BACK
Using 3¼mm needles and A, cast on 72(76,80)sts.
Work 4cm in K1, P1 rib, ending with a right-side row.
Inc row: P11(10,10), ✶ inc in next st, P9(10,11), rep

This spectacular circus cardigan has all the colour and razzmatazz of the Big Top. The eye-catching combination of abstract shapes and bold colours is one that children will adore.

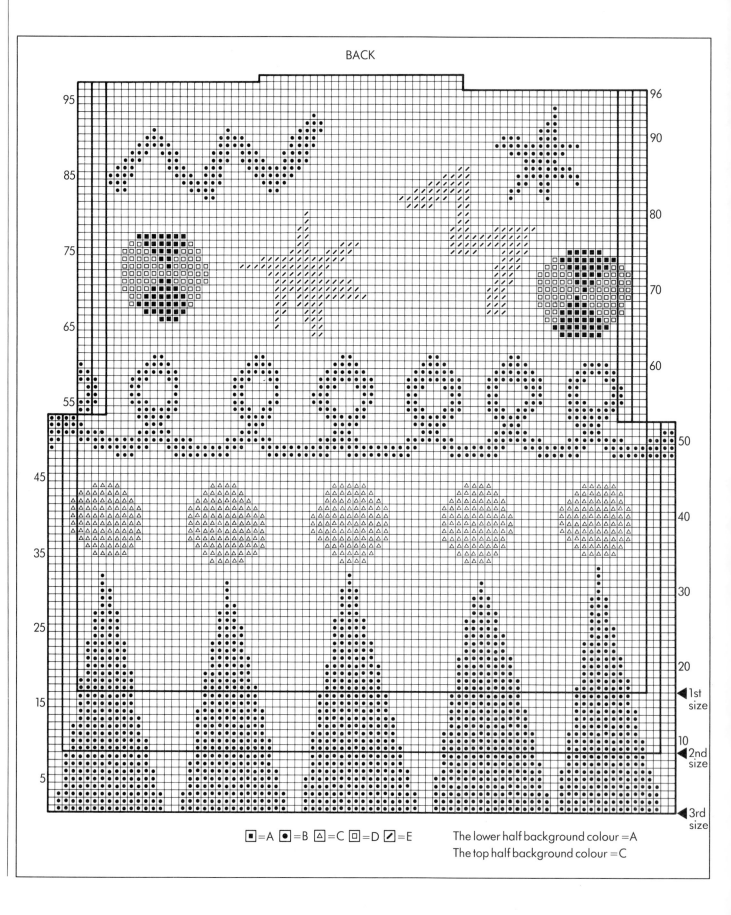

BACK

■=A   ●=B   △=C   ▢=D   ╱=E

The lower half background colour =A
The top half background colour =C

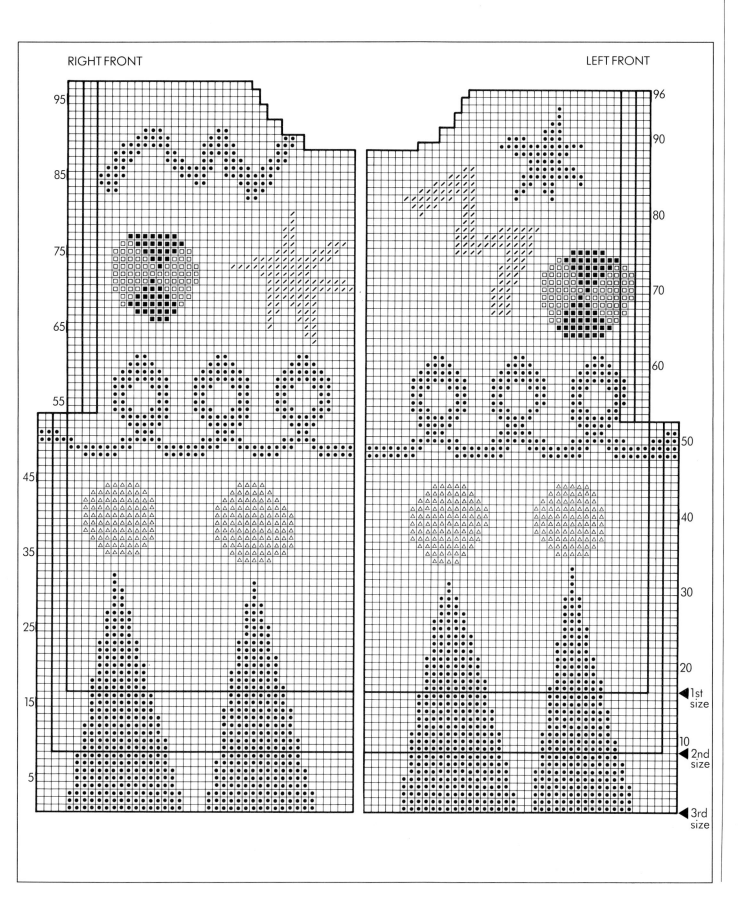

RIGHT FRONT

LEFT FRONT

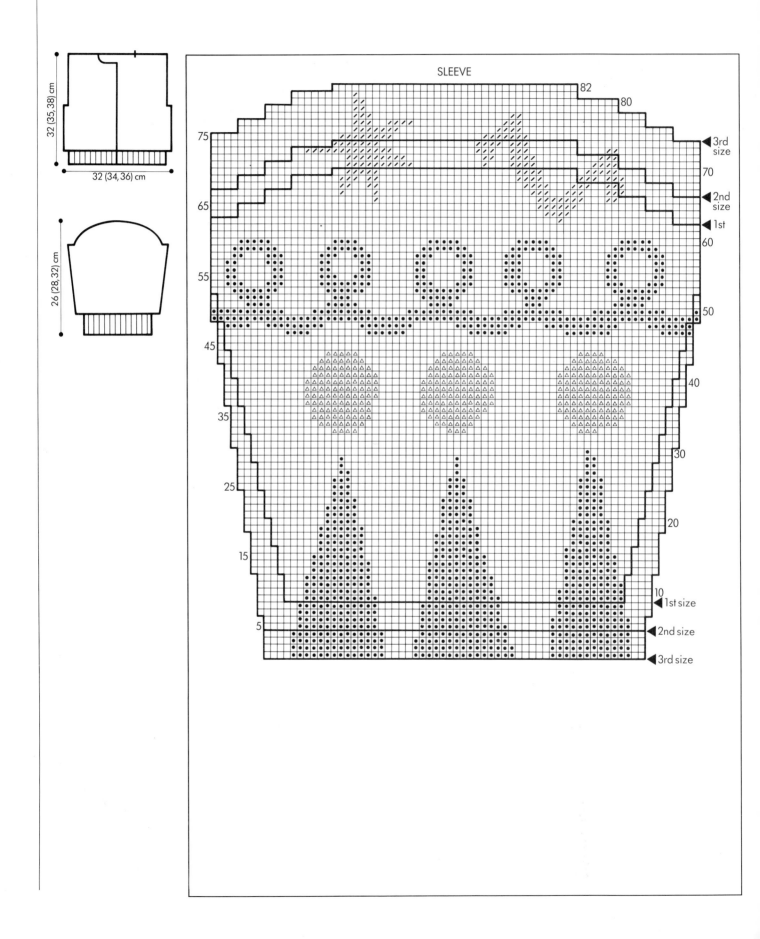

The back of this stunning cardigan is as exciting as the front. Notice that the abstract shapes are not regular, so follow the charts carefully for an exact result.

from ☆ to last 11(11,10)sts, inc in next st, P to end: 78(82,86)sts.
Change to 4mm needles.
Reading odd numbered (K) rows from right to left and even numbered (P) rows from left to right, work in patt from chart for back, working armhole and shoulder shaping as indicated.

RIGHT FRONT

Using 3¼mm needles and A, cast on 36(38,40)sts.
Work 4cm in K1, P1 rib, ending with a right-side row.
Inc row: P8, [inc in next st, P9] twice, inc in next st, P7(9,11): 39(41,43)sts.
Change to 4mm needles.
Work in patt from chart for right front, working armhole and neck shaping as indicated.

LEFT FRONT

Work as given for right front, following chart for left front.

SLEEVES

Using 3¼mm needles and A, cast on 42(48,48)sts.
Work 6cm in K1, P1 rib, ending with a right-side row.
Inc row: P6, ☆ inc in next st, P5(4,4), rep from ☆ to last 6(7,7)sts, inc in next st, P5(6,6): 48(56,56)sts.
Change to 4mm needles.
Work in patt from chart for sleeve, working increases as indicated.

BUTTONHOLE BORDER

With right side facing, using 3¼mm needles and A, pick up and K74(84,94)sts up right front to beg of neck shaping.
Work 3 rows K1, P1 rib.
Buttonhole row: (Right side) Rib 4, ☆ yrn, P2 tog, rib 10(12,14), rep from ☆ to last 8 sts, yrn, P2 tog, rib to end.
Rib 3 more rows.
Cast off in rib.

BUTTON BORDER

Work as given for buttonhole border, picking up sts down left front edge and omitting buttonholes.

NECKBAND

Join shoulder seams.
With right side facing, using 3¼mm needles and A, pick up and K6 sts across buttonhole border, 19 sts up right side of front neck, 28 sts across back neck, 19 sts down left side of front neck, then 6 sts across button border: 78 sts.
Work 3cm in K1, P1 rib.
Cast off in rib.

TO MAKE UP

Sew in sleeves, then join side and sleeve seams. Sew on buttons. Press lightly following instructions on ball band.

MONTY PYTHON

A cuddly toy snake — all five feet of him!

MEASUREMENTS
Length approximately 152cm [60in]
Circumference 20cm

MATERIALS
2 × 50g balls King Cole Superwash 4 ply in main colour A
1 ball same in each of contrast colours B and C
Oddment for mouth in contrast colour D
A pair each of 3mm (No 11) and 3¼mm (No 10) knitting needles
Washable filling

TENSION
32 sts and 40 rows to 10 cm measured over st st worked on 3mm needles

INSTRUCTIONS

TAIL
Using 3mm needles and A, cast on 6 sts.
Working in st st throughout, inc 1 st each end of 7th and every following 6th row until there are 32 sts.
Work 5 rows straight.
Break off yarn, then onto same needle holding the sts, cast on and make a second piece in the same way but do not break off yarn.
Next row: K the first 31 of first set of sts, K tog the last st with the first st of second set of 32 sts, K to end: 63 sts.
Work 7 rows straight.
★ Change to 3¼mm needles and work in patt from chart as follows:
Row 1: K1A, ✢ 2B, 4A, rep from ✢ to last 2 sts, 2B.
Row 2: P3B, ✢ 2A, 4B, rep from ✢ to end.
Continue in patt from chart until row 16 has been completed.
Change to 3mm needles.
Work 12 rows st st in A. ★
The last 28 rows from ★ to ★ form the patt, rep them 13 times more, then the first 16 rows again.
Change to 3mm needles. Work 6 rows in A.
Divide for head shaping
Next row: K30, inc in next st, turn and leave remaining sts on a spare needle: 32 sts.
Work 1 row.
Shape head
★★ Inc 1 st each end of next and every following alternate row until there are 40 sts.
Work 5 rows straight.
Dec 1 st each end of next and every following alternate row until 12 sts remain, ending P row. ★★
Cast off.

Return to remaining sts.
With right side facing, rejoin A to first st and K to end: 32 sts.
Work 1 row.
Now shape head as given for first side from ★★ to ★★.
Break off A and join in D.
Shape mouth lining
Continuing in st st, work 2 rows.
Inc 1 st each end of next and every following alternate row until there are 40 sts.
Work 25 rows straight, so ending with a P row.
Dec 1 st each end of next and every following alternate row until 12 sts remain.
Cast off.

TONGUE
Using 3mm needles and 2 strands of B together, cast on 32 sts.
K 2 rows.
Next row: Cast off 8 sts, K to end. K 1 row.
Next row: Cast on 8 sts, K to end. K 1 row. Cast off.

TO MAKE UP
Swiss darn eyes as given on chart, working them 6 sts apart in line with the mouth. Join cast-off edge of outer head to cast-off sts of lining. Matching patterns, join tail and side seams leaving a small opening for filling. Join lining for mouth to sides of head, fill lightly then catch lining into place at back of throat. Sew in tongue. Fill tail and body, then neatly close opening.

Monty is a cuddly knitted snake that children love to wind around their necks (without the stuffing he could double as a scarf). A loveable toy, he can't bite but is sometimes heard to hiss affectionately!

EYES CHART

28 row patt rep

End   6 st rep   Start

☐ = A   ⦿ = B   ⊡ = C

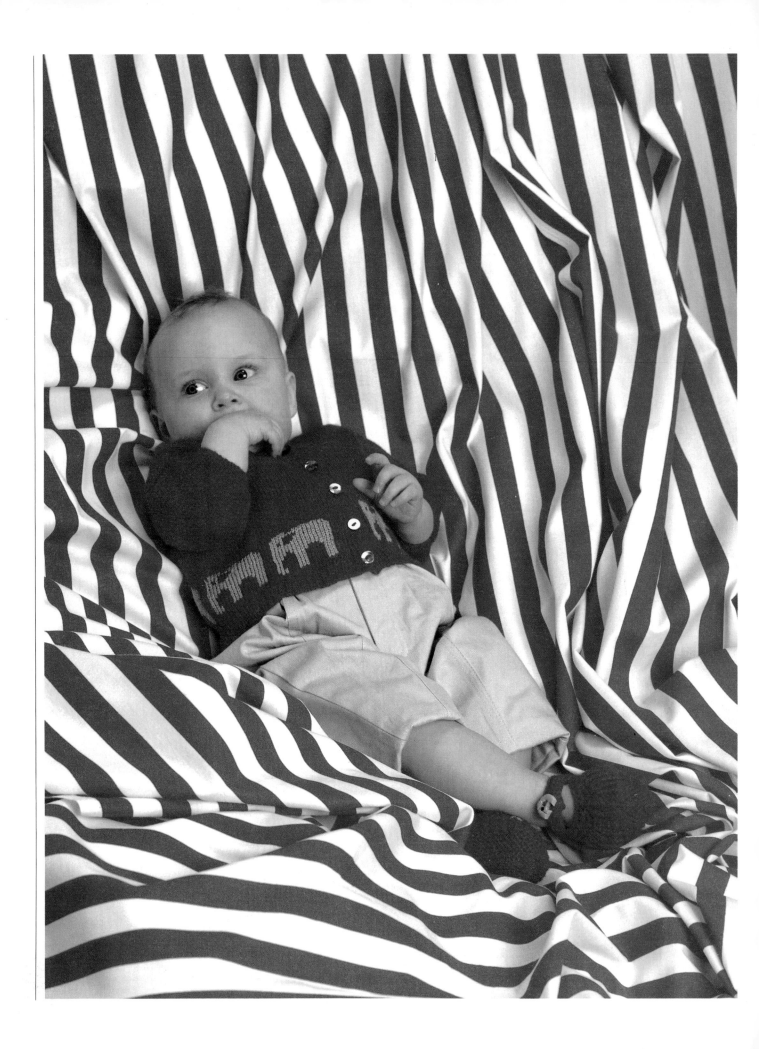

NELLIE THE ELEPHANT

Baby's cardigan with marching elephants around the bottom and matching bootees.

MEASUREMENTS
Cardigan
To fit chest 41–46cm [16–18in]
Actual measurements 51cm
Length to shoulders 25cm
Sleeve seam 13cm
Bootees
To fit 0–6 months

MATERIALS
Cardigan
2 × 50g balls Woolgatherers Tendresse 3 ply in main colour A
1 ball same in contrast colour B
A pair each of 2¼mm (No 13), 3mm (No 11) and 3¼mm (No 10) knitting needles
6 buttons
Bootees
1 ball same in main colour A
2 buttons

TENSION
32 sts and 36 rows to 10cm measured over st st worked on 3mm needles

INSTRUCTIONS FOR CARDIGAN

BACK AND FRONT
(worked in one piece to armholes)
Using 2¼mm needles and A, cast on 177 sts.
Rib row 1: K2, ✫ P1, K1, rep from ✫ to last st, K1.
Rib row 2: K1, ✫ P1, K1, rep from ✫ to end.
Rep these 2 rows twice more.
Next row: (Buttonhole row) K2, P1, yrn, P2 tog, rib to end.
Beg rib row 2, work 3 more rows in rib.
Next row: Rib 7 and slip these sts onto a safety-pin, change to 3mm needles and K to last 7 sts, turn and leave remaining sts on a safety-pin: 163 sts.
Beg P row, work 3 rows st st.
Change to 3¼mm needles.
Work elephant motifs from chart as follows:
Row 1: K3A, [3B, 5A, 3B, 3A, 2B, 4A] 8 times.
Row 2: P3A, [3B, 3A, 3B, 5A, 3B, 3A] 8 times.
Continue in patt from chart until row 16 has been completed. Change to 3mm needles.
Continue in st st until work measures 15cm from beg, ending with a P row.
Divide for back and fronts
Next row: K40 and slip these sts onto a holder for right front, K the next 83 sts, turn and leave remaining 40 sts on a holder for left front.

Working on sts for back, cast off 5 sts at beg of next 2 rows.
Work 1 row.
Next row: K2, K2 tog tbl, K to last 4 sts, K2 tog, K2.
Next row: P.
Rep the last 2 rows until 61 sts remain.
Work straight until back measures 25cm from beg, ending with a P row.
Shape shoulders
Cast off 19 sts at beg of next 2 rows.
Break off yarn and leave remaining 23 sts on a holder.
Return to sts on holder for right front.
With wrong side facing, join on A, cast off 5 sts then P to end: 35 sts.
★ Dec 1 st at armhole edge as given for back on next and every following alternate row until 29 sts remain.
Work straight until front measures 20cm from beg, ending at front edge.
Next row: Work across first 4 sts then slip these sts onto a safety-pin, work to end.
Work 1 row.
Dec 1 st at neck edge on next and every following alternate row until 19 sts remain.
Work straight until front measures same as back to shoulders, ending with a P row.
Cast off. ★
Return to sts on holder for left front.
With right side facing, join on A, cast off 5 sts, then K to end: 35 sts.
Work 1 row.
Now complete as given for right front from ★ to ★.

SLEEVES
Using 2¼mm needles and A, cast on 43 sts.
Work 10 rows rib as given for back and fronts.
Change to 3mm needles.
Inc row: K1, ✫ inc into next st, K1, rep from ✫ to end: 64 sts.
Working in st st, inc 1 st at each end of 11th and every following 10th row until there are 70 sts.
Work straight until sleeve measures 13cm from beg, ending with a P row.
Shape top
Cast off 5 sts at beg of next 2 rows.
Working shaping as given for back, dec 1 st each end of next and every following alternate row until 48 sts remain, ending with a P row.
Cast off 6 sts at beg of next 4 rows: 24 sts.
Cast off.

BUTTON BORDER
With right side facing, slip the 7 sts on holder at lower edge of left front onto a 2¼mm needle, join on A, inc into first st, [K1,P1] twice, K2: 8 sts.
Next row: [K1, P1] 4 times.
Continue in rib until border, when slightly stretched, fits up front to beg of neck shaping. Break off yarn

A delightful cardigan and bootee set featuring marching elephants; the baby's cardigan is hardly jumbo-sized but these boots were made for walking!

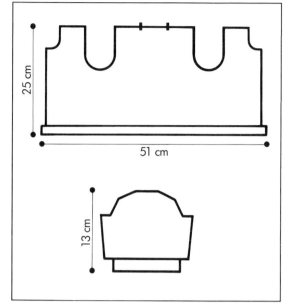

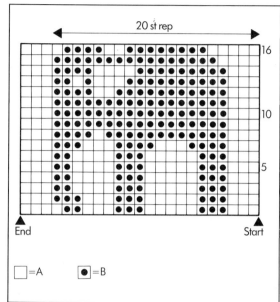

=A   ●=B

and leave sts on holder. Sew on the border and mark the position for 5 buttons, the first one to match first buttonhole, the top one 4cm from top of border and the others spaced evenly in between.

BUTTONHOLE BORDER

With wrong side facing, slip the 7 sts on holder at lower edge of right front onto a 2¼mm needle, join on A, inc into first st, [P1, K1] 3 times.
Next row: K2, [P1, K1] 3 times.
Complete as given for button border, working buttonholes to correspond with markers as follows:
Buttonhole row: (Right side) K2, P1, yrn, P2 tog, K1, P1, K1.

NECKBAND

Sew on buttonhole border and join shoulder seams. With right side facing, using 2¼mm needles and A, rib across 7 sts of buttonhole border, K the last st of buttonhole border together with first of 4 sts on safety-pin at right front neck, K the next 3 sts, pick up and K16 sts up right front neck, K across 23 sts from back neck holder, pick up and K16 sts down left front neck, K 3 sts from safety-pin at left front and K the last st on safety-pin together with first st from button border, then rib 7: 77 sts.
Next row: (Wrong side) K1, * P1, K1, rep from * to end.
Buttonhole row: K2, P1, yrn, P2 tog, rib to end.
Work 11 more rows rib, making a second buttonhole on the eighth row. Cast off in rib.

TO MAKE UP

Fold neckband in half to wrong side and slipstitch into position. Join sleeve seams, then sew in sleeves. Press lightly following instructions on ball band.

INSTRUCTIONS FOR BOOTEES

Using 3¼mm needles and 2 strands of yarn together throughout, cast on 31 sts.
K 1 row.
Shape sole as follows:
Row 1: (Right side) Inc in first st, K14, inc in next st, K14, inc in last st.
Row 2 and every alternate row: K to end.
Row 3: Inc in first st, K15, inc in next st, K16, inc in last st.
Row 5: Inc in first st, K17, inc in next st, K17, inc in last st.
Row 7: Inc in first st, K18, inc in next st, K19, inc in last st.
Row 9: Inc in first st, K20, inc in next st, K20, inc in last st.
Row 11: Inc in first st, K21, inc in next st, K22, inc in last st: 49 sts.
Row 12: K to end.
Work in patt as follows:
Row 1: (Right side) K1, * yf, sl 1 pw, yon, K1, rep from * to end.
Row 2: K1, K2 tog, * yf, sl 1 pw, yon, K2 tog, rep from * to last st, K1.
Row 3: K1, * yf, sl 1 pw, yon, K2 tog, rep from * to last 2 sts, yf, sl 1 pw, yon, K1.
Rep rows 2 and 3 five times more, then work row 2 again.
Next row: (Right side) K2, * K2 tog, K1, rep from * to last 4 sts, K2 tog, K2.
Next row: K20, [K2 tog] twice, K1, [K2 tog] twice, K20.
Next row: K18, [K2 tog] twice, K1, [K2 tog] twice, K18.
Next row: K16, [K2 tog] twice, K1, [K2 tog] twice, K16.

"Nellie the elephant packed her trunk,
And trundled off to the circus,
Off she went with a trumpetty trump,
Trump, trump, trump.

Night by night, she danced to the circus band,
When Nellie was leading the big parade
She looked so proud and grand.

No more tricks for Nellie to perform,
They taught her how to take a bow
And she took the crowd by storm.

Nellie the elephant packed her trunk,
And trundled back to the jungle,
Off she went with a trumpetty trump,
Trump, trump, trump."

Next row: K14, [K2 tog] twice, K1, [K2 tog] twice, K14: 33 sts.
Next row: K10, cast off 13 sts, K to end.
Work on first set of 10 sts for button strap.
Next row: K to end.
Next row: Cast on 8 sts, K to end: 18 sts. K 3 rows. (For 2nd bootee, work buttonhole on first of these rows.)
Cast off.
With right side facing, join yarn to remaining 10 sts, cast on 8 sts, then K to end: 18 sts.

K 1 row.
Next row: (Buttonhole row) K3, yrn, skpo, K to end. (For 2nd bootee, K this row.)
K 2 rows.
Cast off.
Make 2nd bootee in same way, reversing buttonhole on strap as indicated.

TO MAKE UP
Join sole and centre back seam.
Sew on buttons.

HARLEQUIN

A colourful long-sleeved raglan jumper with a cheeky stand-up collar.

MEASUREMENTS

To fit chest 46(51,56)cm [18(20,22)in]
Actual measurements 56(61,66)cm
Length to shoulders 27·5(30,33·5)cm
Sleeve seam 18(20,23)cm

MATERIALS

1 × 50g ball King Cole Superwash 4 ply in each of colours A, B, C and D
A pair each of 2¼mm (No 13) and 3mm (No11) knitting needles and one 2¼mm (No 13) circular needle

TENSION

32 sts and 40 rows to 10cm measured over st st worked on 3mm needles

INSTRUCTIONS

BACK

★ Using 2¼mm needles and B, cast on 91(99,107)sts.
Rib row 1: K2, ★ P1, K1, rep from ★ to last st, K1.
Rib row 2: K1, ★ P1, K1, rep from ★ to end.
Rep these 2 rows for 4cm, ending with rib row 2 and increasing 1 st at end of last row: 92(100,108)sts.
Change to 3mm needles. Break off B and join in D.
Beg with a K row, work in st st until back measures 15(16·5,19)cm from beg, ending with a P row.
Shape raglans
Cast off 4 sts at beg of next 2 rows.
Work 2 rows straight. ★
Next row: K2, K2 tog, K to last 4 sts, skpo, K2.
Next row: P.
Rep these 2 rows until 36(40,44) sts remain, ending with a P row.
Break off yarn and leave sts on a holder.

FRONT

Using A instead of B and C instead of D, work as given for back from ★ to ★.
Next row: K2, K2 tog, K to last 4 sts, skpo, K2.
Next row: P.
Rep these 2 rows until 54(58,62) sts remain, ending with a P row.
Shape neck
Next row: K2, K2 tog, K16, turn and leave remaining sts on a spare needle.
Continuing to dec at raglan edge as before, dec 1 st at neck edge on next 8 rows.
Keeping neck edge straight, dec at raglan edge as before until 3 sts remain. Cast off.
Return to remaining sts.

With right side facing, slip the first 14(18,22)sts onto a holder, join on C and complete second side of neck to match first, reversing all shaping.

SLEEVES

Using 2¼mm needles and D for right sleeve or C for left sleeve, cast on 53(53,61)sts.
Work 4cm rib as given for back, increasing 1 st at end of last row: 54(54,62) sts.
Change to 3mm needles.
Break off yarn and join on A for right sleeve or B for left sleeve.
Beg K row, work in st st, increasing 1 st each end of 5th and every following 4th row to 62(62,68)sts, then every following 6th row until there are 74(74,82)sts.
Work straight until sleeve measures 18(20,23)cm from beg, ending with a P row.
Shape raglan
Cast off 4 sts at beg of next 2 rows.
Next row: K2, K2 tog, K to last 4 sts, skpo, K2.
Next row: P.
Rep these 2 rows until 14(14,18)sts remain, ending P row.
Break off yarn and leave sts on a holder.

COLLAR

Join raglan seams.
With right side facing, slip the first 7(9,11)sts from holder at centre front neck onto a safety-pin, using the circular needle and A, K across remaining 7(9,11)sts from holder, pick up and K18 sts up right side of neck, K across 14(14,18)sts from right sleeve holder, 36(40,44)sts from back neck holder and 14(14,18)sts from left sleeve holder, pick up and K19 sts down left side of neck, then K across 7(9,11)sts from safety-pin: 116(124,140)sts.
Round 1: K1, ★ P1, K1, rep from ★ to end. (Forming K2 at centre front.)
Rep this round for 2cm.
Now continue in rows as follows:
Row 1: K1, ★ P1, K1, rep from ★ to end, turn.
Row 2: K2, ★ P1, K1, rep from ★ to last st, K1, turn.
Continue working backwards and forwards in rows until collar measures 5cm from beg, ending with a wrong-side row.
Cast off knitwise.

TO MAKE UP

Join side and sleeve seams. Press lightly following instructions on ball band.

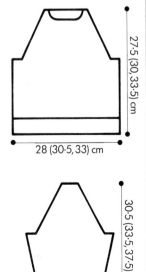

27·5 (30,33·5) cm

28 (30·5, 33) cm

30·5 (33·5, 37·5) cm

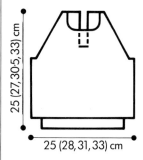

25 (27,30·5,33) cm

25 (28, 31, 33) cm

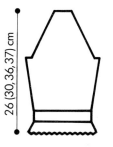

26 (30,36,37) cm

PIERROT

A slightly fluffy raglan jumper with an all-in-one ruff at the neck, frills at the cuffs and spots or pompons down the front.

MEASUREMENTS
To fit chest 41 (46,51,56)cm [16(18,20,22)in]
Actual measurements 50(56,62,66)cm
Length to shoulders 25(27,30·5,33)cm
Sleeve seam 15(18,22,23)cm

MATERIALS
1(2,3,3) × 50g balls Phildar Anouchka in main colour A
1 ball same in contrast colour B
A pair each of 2¼mm (No 13) and 3mm (No 11) knitting needles
3 buttons

TENSION
28 sts and 36 rows to 10cm measured over st st worked on 3mm needles

INSTRUCTIONS

BACK
Using 2¼mm needles and B, cast on 67(75,81,87) sts.
Row 1: K2, * P1, K1, rep from * to last st, K1.
Break off B and join on A.
Row 2: K1, P to last st, K1.
Row 3: K2, * P1, K1, rep from * to last st, K1.
Row 4: K1, * P1, K1, rep from * to end.
Rep rows 3 and 4 until work measures 2·5(2·5,4,4)cm from beg, ending with row 3.
Inc row: Rib 14(16, 10, 8), [inc in next st, rib 11(13,11,13)sts] 3(3,5,5) times, inc in next st, rib to end: 71(79,87,93) sts.
Change to 3mm needles.
Beg K row, work in st st until back measures 14(15, 16·5,19) cm from beg, ending with a P row.
Shape raglans
Cast off 2(3,3,4) sts at beg of next 2 rows.
Next row: K2, K2 tog, K to last 4 sts, skpo, K2.
Next row: P.
Rep last 2 rows until 57(59,61,65) sts remain, ending with a P row.
Divide for back opening
Next row: K2, K2 tog, K22(23,24,26), turn and leave remaining sts on a spare needle.
Keeping neck edge straight, continue dec at raglan edge as before until 11(12,13,15) sts remain.
Break off yarn and leave sts on a holder.
Return to remaining sts.
With right side facing, join on yarn and cast off the first 5 sts, K to last 4 sts, skpo., K2.

Black and white used to be considered far too severe for babies and small children. But these original Pierrot jumpers look stunning on small children even though they call, quite naturally, for solid black accessories.

Now complete second side of neck to match first, reversing all shaping.

FRONT
Work as given for back until 41(43,45,49) sts remain when shaping raglans.
Shape neck
Next row: K2, K2 tog, K13, turn and leave remaining sts on a spare needle.
Decreasing at raglan edge as before, dec 1 st at neck edge on next 8 rows.
Keeping neck edge straight, continue dec at raglan edge until 2 sts remain. Cast off.
Return to remaining sts.
With right side facing, slip first 7(9,11,15) sts onto a holder, join on yarn and complete to match first side of neck, reversing all shaping.

SLEEVES
For 1st size only
Using 2¼mm needles and B, cast on 39 sts and work rows 1 and 2 as given for back.
For 2nd, 3rd and 4th sizes only
Using 3mm needles and B, cast on (82,86,94) sts.
K1 row.
Break off B and join on A.
Beg with a K row, work 7 rows st st.
Next row: * P2 tog, rep from * to end: (41,43,47) sts.
Change to 2¼mm needles.
All sizes
Rep rows 3 and 4 as given for back 5(5,6,6) times.
Change to 3mm needles.
Working in st st, inc 1 st each end of 5th(1st,1st,5th) and every following 4th row until there are 55(61,67,71) sts.
Work straight until sleeve measures 15(18,22,23)cm from beg, ending with a P row.
Shape raglan
Cast off 2(3,3,4) sts at beg of next 2 rows.
Next row: K2, K2 tog, K to last 4 sts, skpo, K2.
Next row: P.
Rep these 2 rows until 11(11,11,13) sts remain, ending with a P row.
Break off yarn and leave sts on a holder.

FRILL
For 2nd, 3rd and 4th sizes only
Using 3mm needles and B, cast on (166,174,198) sts.
K1 row.
Break off B and join on A.
Beg with a K row, work 12 rows st st.
Next row: * K2 tog, rep from * to end of row: (83,87,99) sts.
Break off yarn and leave sts on needle.

NECKBAND
Join raglan seams.
With right side facing and using 2¼mm needles and

SPOT CHART

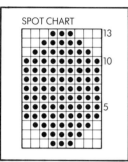

A, K across 11(12,13,15) sts from left back holder and 11(11,11,13) sts from left sleeve, pick up and K14 sts down left front neck, K across 7(9,11,15) sts from front neck holder, pick up and K14 sts up right front neck, then K across 11(11,11,13) sts from right sleeve holder and 11(12,13,15) sts from right back holder: 79(83,87,99) sts.

1st size only
Using B, P 1 row.
Next row: K2, * P1, K1, rep from * to last st, K1.
Break off B.
Continuing in A, P1 row.

2nd, 3rd and 4th sizes only
Holding wrong side of frill to right side of neck, P together 1 st from neckband with 1 st from frill to end of row: (83,87,99) sts.

All sizes
Rib row 1: K2, * P1, K1, rep from * to last st, K1.
Rib row 2: K1, * P1, K1, rep from * to end.
Rep these 2 rows 3(6, 6, 6) times more.
Cast off in rib.

BUTTONHOLE BORDER
With right side facing and using 2¼mm needles and A, pick up and K33(35,35,35) sts evenly down right back opening.
Row 1: K2, * P1, K1, rep from * to last st, K1.
Row 2: K1, * P1, K1, rep from * to end.
Row 3: As row 1.
Row 4: Keeping rib correct, rib 5, [yrn, skpo, rib 8] twice, yrn, skpo, rib 6(8,8,8).
Rows 5 and 6: As rows 1 and 2.
Row 7: As row 1.
Cast off purlwise.

BUTTON BORDER
Work as given for buttonhole border, omitting buttonholes.

TO MAKE UP
Stitch row ends of button and buttonhole borders into place over cast-off sts. Fold neckband in half to wrong side and slipstitch into position. Sew on buttons. Join side and sleeve seams. Press lightly following instructions on ball band.
For 1st size only
Placing motifs centrally as shown and using B, Swiss darn spots to front of sweater.
For 2nd, 3rd and 4th sizes only
Using B, make 2 pompons (see page 141) approximately 4·5cm in size and stitch securely into place on front of sweater.

PIERROT DOLL

Pierrot himself — a knitted doll with separate costume, that is easy to put on and take off.

MEASUREMENTS
Height approximately 33cm [13in]

MATERIALS
Doll
1 × 50g ball 4 ply yarn in main colour A
Oddments of 4 ply in Black for feet, hat and eyes and Red for nose and mouth
Pierrot Costume
1 × 50g ball Phildar Anouchka in main colour A
Oddments in Black for edgings and pompons
1 button
A pair of 3mm (No 11) knitting needles
3.00mm crochet hook
Washable filling
Shirring elastic

TENSION
Doll
26 sts and 36 rows to 10cm measured over st st using 3mm needles and 4 ply
Pierrot Costume
28 sts and 36 rows to 10cm measured over st st using 3mm needles and Anouchka

INSTRUCTIONS FOR DOLL

HEAD
Using 3mm needles and A, cast on 16 sts, P 1 row.
Shape head as follows:
Row 1: (Right side) * inc in next st, K1, rep from * to end: 24 sts.
Row 2: K1, P to last st, K1.
Rep these 2 rows twice more: 54 sts.
Continue in st st, without shaping, until work measures 7·5cm from beg, ending with a P row.
Shape neck
Row 1: [K1, K2 tog] 9 times, [K2 tog, K1] 9 times.
Row 2: K1, P to last st, K1.
Row 3: [K1, K2 tog] 6 times, [K2 tog, K1] 6 times.
Row 4: As row 2.
Row 5: [K1, K2 tog] 4 times, [K2 tog, K1] 4 times.
Row 6: K1, P to last st, K1: 16 sts.
Work 4 rows straight.
Shape body
Row 1: * Inc in next st, K1, rep from * to end: 24 sts.
Row 2: K1, P to last st, K1.
Rep these 2 rows twice more: 54 sts.
Work straight for 11·5cm, ending with a P row.
Divide for legs
Next row: K27, turn and leave remaining sts on a spare needle.

★ Work straight until leg measures 7·5cm, ending with a P row.
Shape ankle
Next row: ✳ K1, K2 tog, rep from ✳ to end: 18 sts.
P 1 row.
Break off A, join in black.
K 2 rows.
Beg K row, work 6 rows st st. ★
Shape foot
Next row: K8, turn and P4, turn and work 4 rows st st on these 4 sts, so ending with a P row.
Now K across the 4 sts, pick up and K3 sts down side of the 4 rows of st st, then K across remaining 10 sts: 17 sts.
Next row: P17, pick up and P3 sts down second side of 4 rows, then P remaining 4 sts: 24 sts.
Work 2 rows st st, then K 3 rows.
Cast off knitwise. Return to remaining sts.
With right side facing, rejoin A to first st and work as given for first leg from ★ to ★.
Shape foot
Next row: K14, turn and P4, turn and work 4 rows st st on these 4 sts, so ending P row.
Now complete as for first leg, reversing all shaping.

ARMS
Using 3mm needles and A, cast on 8 sts for shoulder.
Working in st st, inc 1 st each end of every row until there are 18 sts.
Work straight until arm measures 11·5cm from beg, ending with a P row.
Next row: ✳ K2 tog, rep from ✳ to end of row: 9 sts.
Break off yarn and thread through sts, draw up tightly and fasten off securely.

HAT
Using 3¼mm needles and black, cast on 56 sts.
K 5 rows.
Beg K row, work 16 rows st st.
Shape crown
Row 1: ✳ K2 tog, rep from ✳ to end: 28 sts.
Row 2: P to end.
Rep these 2 rows once more: 14 sts.
Break off yarn and thread through sts, draw up tightly and fasten off securely.

TO MAKE UP
Using back stitch and black, embroider the outer line of eyes onto face. Working from chart, Swiss darn centre of eyes, eyebrows, nose and mouth onto face.
Join feet and leg seams, then head, neck and back leaving a small opening. Turn body to right side, fill as firmly as required, then close opening. Join arm seams, turn to right side then fill as required and sew into place. Join seam at back of hat, then slipstitch onto head.

INSTRUCTIONS FOR PIERROT COSTUME

FRONT
★ Using 3mm needles and black, cast on 25 sts for right leg.
K 1 row.
Break off black and join in A.
Beg K row, work in st st until leg measures 7.5cm, ending with a P row.
Break off yarn and leave sts on a spare needle.
Work left leg in same way but do not break off yarn.
Next row: K25 sts of left leg, then K25 sts of right leg from spare needle: 50 sts.
Beg P row, work in st st until front measures 18cm from beg, ending with a P row.
Shape raglans
Cast off 2 sts at beg of next 2 rows: 46 sts. ★
Next row: K2, K2 tog, K to last 4 sts, K2 tog tbl, K2.
Next row: P to end.
Rep these 2 rows until 10 sts remain, ending with a P row.
Break off yarn and leave sts on a holder.

BACK
Work as given for front from ★ to ★.
Divide for back opening
Next row: K2, K2 tog, K19, turn and leave remaining sts on a spare needle.
Next row: P to end.
Next row: K2, K2 tog, K to end.
Rep these last 2 rows until 5 sts remain, ending with a P row.
Break off yarn and leave sts on a holder.

This is the smallest size of the Pierrot jumper just to prove that small babies can wear black too. But, for a baby, add Swiss-darned spots instead of pompons – they are much harder to chew!

Practical cotton is a good choice for this mini tracksuit which is perfect for crawling about in. Swiss-darn the balloon motif all over for a thoroughly dotty effect.

Return to remaining sts.
With right side facing, join on A, K to last 4 sts, K2 tog tbl, K2.
Next row: P to end.
Next row: K to last 4 sts, K2 tog tbl, K2.
Rep these last 2 rows until 5 sts remain, ending with a P row.
Break off yarn and leave sts on a holder.

SLEEVES

Using 3mm needles and black, cast on 46 sts.
K 1 row.
Break off black and join in A.
Beg K row, work 6 rows st st.
Next row: * K2 tog, rep from * to end: 23 sts.
Now work in rib as follows:
Rib row 1: K1, * P1, K1, rep. from * to end.
Rib row 2: K2, * P1, K1, rep. from * to last st, K1.
Rep these 2 rows once more, then rib row 1 again.
Inc row: K into back and front of each st to end: 46 sts.
Next row: P to end.
Beg K row, work in st st until sleeve measures 7·5cm from beg, ending with a P row.
Shape raglan
Cast off 2 sts at beg of next 2 rows: 42 sts.
Now dec as given for front until 6 sts remain, ending with a P row.
Break off yarn and leave sts on a holder.

FRILL

Using 3mm needles and black, cast on 64 sts.
K 1 row.
Break off black and join in A.
Beg K row, work 12 rows st st.
Next row: * K2 tog, rep from * to end: 32 sts.
Break off yarn and leave sts on needle.

NECKBAND

Join raglan seams.
With right side facing and using 3mm needles and A, K across the 5 sts on holder at left back neck, 6 sts from left sleeve, 10 sts across front, 6 sts from right sleeve and 5 sts from right back neck: 32 sts.
Now holding wrong side of frill to right side of neck, P together 1 st from neckband with 1 st from frill to end of row: 32 sts.
Work 4 rows K1, P1 rib. Cast off knitwise.

TO MAKE UP

Join leg, side and sleeve seams. Join inside leg seams. Using 3·00mm crochet hook and A, work 2 rows double crochet round neck opening, working a button loop at top of right back neck.
Sew on button. Using black, make 2 small pompons (see page 141), approximately 2 cm across and stitch to front as shown. Thread wrists and ankles with shirring elastic and gather slightly.

BALLOONS

Spotted tracksuits for baby and bear!

MEASUREMENTS
Child's tracksuit
To fit chest 51cm [20in]
Actual measurements 56cm
Length to shoulders 32cm
Sleeve seam 20cm
Outside leg (waist to ankle) 54cm
Teddy's tracksuit
To fit height 48cm [19in]

MATERIALS
Child's tracksuit
13 × 50g balls Rowan D.K. cotton in main colour A
Teddy's tracksuit
4 × 25g balls Rowan lightweight D.K. in main colour A
2 balls same in contrast colour B
For both suits
Oddments of 4 contrasting colours for Swiss-darned spots
A pair each of 3¾mm (No 9) and 4½mm (No7) knitting needles for child's and a pair of 3¼mm (No 10) knitting needles for teddy's tracksuit
3 buttons for each tracksuit
Waist length of elastic for each tracksuit

TENSION
20 sts and 28 rows to 10cm measured over st st worked on 4½mm needles with cotton
22 sts and 28 rows to 10cm measured over st st worked on 4½mm needles with lightweight wool

INSTRUCTIONS FOR CHILD'S TRACKSUIT

BACK
Using 3¾mm needles cast on 50 sts.
Rib row: * K1 tb1, P1, rep from * to end.
Rep this row 10 times more to form twisted rib.
Inc row: Rib 8, * M1, rib 7, rep from * to end: 56 sts.
Change to 4½mm needles.
Beg K row, work in st st until back measures 32cm from beg, ending with a P row.
Shape shoulders
Cast off 18 sts at beg of next 2 rows.
Break off yarn and leave remaining 20 sts on a holder.

FRONT
Work as given for back until 12 rows less than back to shoulders have been worked.
Shape neck
Next row: K22, K2 tog, turn and leave remaining sts on a holder.

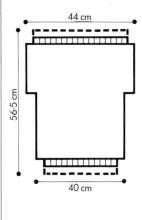

44 cm

56·5 cm

40 cm

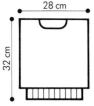

28 cm

32 cm

28 cm

20 cm

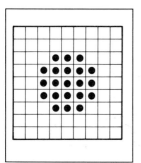

Next row: P2 tog, P to end.
Next row: K to last 2 sts, K2 tog.
Rep the last 2 rows once more: 19 sts.
Next row: P to end.
Next row: K to last 2 sts, K2 tog: 18 sts.
Next row: P.
Beg K row, work 4 rows st st.
Cast off.
Return to remaining sts.
With right side facing, slip first 8 sts onto a holder, join on yarn, K2 tog, K to end: 23 sts.
Now complete to match first side of neck, reversing all shaping.

SLEEVES

Using 3¾mm needles cast on 30 sts.
Work 11 rows in twisted rib as given for back.
Inc row: K2, [M1, K1] 26 times, K2: 56 sts.
Change to 4½mm needles.
Beg K row, work in st st until sleeve measures 20cm from beg, ending with a P row. Cast off.

NECKBAND

Join right shoulder seam.
With right side facing and using 3¾mm needles, pick up and K12 sts down left side of front neck, K across 8 sts from front neck holder, pick up and K12 sts up right side of front neck, then K across 20 sts from back neck holder: 52 sts.
Work 12 rows in twisted rib as given for back.
Cast off in rib.
Fold neckband in half to wrong side and slipstitch into position.

BUTTON BORDER

With right side facing and using 3¾mm needles, pick up and K22 sts across left shoulder and neckband edge.
Work 5 rows in twisted rib.
Cast off in rib.

BUTTONHOLE BORDER

Work as given for button border, placing 3 buttonholes on the 3rd row as follows:
Buttonhole row: (Wrong side) Rib 1, [K2 tog, yf, rib 6] twice, K2 tog, yf, rib 3.

TO MAKE UP

Overlap buttonhole border over button border and catch together at shoulders. Fold sleeves in half, then placing centre of top of sleeves to shoulder seams, sew into position. Working from chart, Swiss-darn spot motifs as required. Join side and sleeve seams. Sew on buttons.

TROUSERS

Right leg: Using 3¾mm needles cast on 40 sts.
Work 6cm in twisted rib, ending with a right-side row.

Inc row: K into back and front of each st to end: 80 sts.
Change to 4½mm needles.
Beg K row, work in st st until leg measures 32cm from beg, ending with a P row.
Shape crutch
Cast on 4 sts at beg of next 2 rows: 88 sts.
Continue in st st until work measures 57cm from beg, ending with a K row.
Next row: (Dec row) Sl 1, * P2 tog, P1, rep from * to end: 59 sts.
Change to 3¾mm needles.
Rib row 1: K1 tb1, * P1, K1 tb1, rep from * to end.
Rib row 2: P1, * K1 tb1, P1, rep from * to end.
Rep these 2 rows for 5cm, ending with rib row 2.
Cast off in rib.
Left leg: Work as given for right leg.

TO MAKE UP

Working from chart, Swiss-darn spot motifs as required. Join front, back and inner leg seams. Fold ribbing at lower edge of legs to wrong side and slipstitch into place. Fold hem at top of trousers in half to wrong side and slipstitch into place, leaving a small opening for elastic. Thread elastic into waistband, secure ends, then close opening.

INSTRUCTIONS FOR TEDDY'S TRACKSUIT

BACK

Using 3¼mm needles and B, cast on 46 sts.
Rib row: * K1 tb1, P1, rep from * to end.
Rep this row 6 times more to form twisted rib.
Inc row: Rib 6, * M1, rib 4, rep from * to end: 56 sts.
Break off B and join in A.
Change to 4½mm needles.
Beg K row, work in st st until back measures 18cm from beg, ending with a P row.
Shape shoulders
Cast off 18 sts at beg of next 2 rows.
Break off yarn and leave remaining 20 sts on a holder.

FRONT

Work as given for back until 12 rows less than back to shoulders have been worked.
Shape neck
Next row: K22, K2 tog, turn and leave remaining sts on a holder.
Next row: P2 tog, P to end.
Next row: K to last 2 sts, K2 tog.
Rep the last 2 rows once more: 19 sts.
Next row: P to end.
Next row: K to last 2 sts, K2 tog: 18 sts.
Next row: P.
Beg K row, work 4 rows st st.
Cast off.
Return to remaining sts.

With right side facing, slip first 8 sts onto a holder, join on yarn, K2 tog, K to end: 23 sts.
Now complete to match first side of neck, reversing all shaping.

SLEEVES

Using 3¼mm needles and B, cast on 28 sts.
Work 3 rows in twisted rib as given for back.
Inc row: K3, [M1, K1] 22 times, K3: 50 sts.
Break off B and join in A.
Change to 4½mm needles.
Beg K row, work in st st until sleeve measures 7·5cm from beg, ending with a P row.
Break off A and join in B. K 3 rows. Cast off.

NECKBAND

Join right shoulder seam.
With right side facing and using 3¼mm needles and B, pick up and K14 sts down left side of front neck, K across 8 sts from front neck holder, pick up and K14 sts up right side of front neck, then K across 20 sts from back neck holder: 56 sts.
K 1 row, then work 10 rows in twisted rib as given for back.
Cast off in rib.
Fold neckband in half to wrong side and slipstitch into position.

BUTTON BORDER

With right side facing and using 3¼mm needles and B, pick up and K22 sts across left shoulder and neckband edge.
K 1 row, then work 45 rows in twisted rib.
Cast off in rib.

BUTTONHOLE BORDER

Work as given for button border, placing 3 buttonholes on the 3rd row as follows:
Buttonhole row: (Wrong side) Rib 1, [K2 tog, yf, rib 6] twice, K2 tog, yf, rib 3.

TO MAKE UP

Overlap buttonhole border over button border and catch together at shoulders. Fold sleeves in half, then placing centre of top of sleeves to shoulder seams, sew into position. Working from chart, Swiss-darn spot motifs as required. Join side and sleeve seams. Sew on buttons.

TROUSERS

Right leg: Using 3¼mm needles and B, cast on 48 sts.
Work 4cm in twisted rib, ending with a wrong-side row.
Break off B.
Join in main yarn A.
Change to 4½mm needles.
Beg K row, work in st st until leg measures 16cm from beg, ending with a P row.

Shape crutch
Cast on 5 sts at beg of next 2 rows: 58 sts.
Continue in st st until work measures 25cm from beg, ending with a P row.
Break off A and join in B.
Change to 3¼mm needles.
Work 4cm in twisted rib.
Cast off in rib.
Left leg: Work as given for right leg.

TO MAKE UP

Working from chart, Swiss-darn spot motifs as required. Join front, back and inner leg seams. Fold ribbing at lower edge of legs to wrong side and slipstitch into place. Fold hem at top of trousers in half to wrong side and slipstitch into place, leaving a small opening for elastic. Thread elastic into waistband, secure ends, then close opening.

Teddy's tracksuit has been designed in a lightweight double knitting woollen yarn but oddments of cotton from the child's tracksuit could easily be substituted. If you change the yarn remember to check the tension.

POCKETS TOP

A chunky little sweater, with a wide collar and lots of little pockets for circus animals and a clown.

MEASUREMENTS
To fit chest 56cm [22in]
Actual measurements 61cm
Length to shoulders 32cm
Sleeve seam 22cm

MATERIALS
5 × 50g balls of Yarn Works Merino Sport in main colour A
1 ball each of same in contrast colours B, C and D
Oddments of Double Knitting in Purple, Orange, Pink, Yellow, Red and Blue for toys
Washable filling for toys
A pair each of 4mm (No 8), 4½mm (No 7) and 5½mm (No 5) knitting needles
2 buttons

TENSION
17 sts and 24 rows to 10cm measured over st st worked on 5½mm needles

INSTRUCTIONS FOR JUMPER

POCKET LININGS (make 4)
Using 5½mm needles and A, cast on 12 sts.
Work 12 rows st st.
Break off yarn and leave sts on a holder.

BACK
★ Using 4½mm needles and B, cast on 44 sts.
Rib row: ✶ K1 tbl, P1, rep from ✶ to end.
Change to A and rep the rib row 10 times more. ★
Inc row: Rib 8, ✶ inc in next st, rib 3, rep from ✶ to last 8 sts, inc in next st, rib to end: 52 sts.
Change to 5½mm needles.
Beg K row, work 66 rows st st.
Cast off 16 sts at beg of next 2 rows.
Break off yarn and leave remaining 20 sts on a holder.

FRONT
Work as given for back from ★ to ★.
Inc row: Rib 6, ✶ inc in next st, rib 3, rep from ✶ to last 6 sts, inc in next st, rib to end: 53sts.
Change to 5½mm needles.
Beg K row, work 4 rows st st.
Using separate small balls of wool for each area of colour and twisting yarns together on wrong side of work when changing colour to avoid making a hole, work coloured pocket as follows:
Next row: K33A, 12C, 8A.
Next row: P8A, 12C, 33A.

Rep these 2 rows 5 times more.
Break off C.
Next row: Using A only, K33, slip the next 12 sts in C onto a holder, then with right side facing K across the 12 sts of one pocket lining, K to end: 53 sts.
Beg P row, work 14 rows st st.
Next row: P35A, 12B, 6A.
Next row: K6A, 12B, 35A.
Rep these 2 rows 5 times more.
Break off B.
Next row: Using A only, P35, slip the next 12 sts in B onto a holder, then with wrong side facing P across the 12 sts of second pocket lining, P to end: 53 sts.
Work 2 rows st st, so ending with a P row.
Divide for neck opening
Next row: K24 then slip these sts onto a holder, cast off the next 5 sts, then K to end: 24 sts.
Beg P row, work 9 rows st st.
Shape neck
Row 1: Cast off 3 sts, work to end.
Row 2: Work to end.
Row 3: Work 2 tog, work to end.
Row 4: Work to last 2 sts, work 2 tog.
Rows 5 and 6: As rows 3 and 4.
Row 7: As row 3.
Row 8: Work to end: 16 sts.
Work 2 rows straight, then cast off.
Return to remaining sts.
With wrong side facing, join A to first st and P to end.
Beg K row, work 9 rows st st.
Now complete 2nd side of neck to match first, reversing all shaping.

RIGHT SLEEVE
Using 4½mm needles and B, cast on 28 sts.
Changing to A on the 2nd row, work 9 rows rib as given for back.
Inc row: Rib 4, ✶ inc in next st, rep from ✶ to last 4 sts, rib to end: 48 sts.
Change to 5½mm needles.
Beg K row, work 10 rows st st.
Place pocket as follows:
Next row: K18A, 12B, 18A.
Next row: P18A, 12B, 18A.
Rep these 2 rows 5 times more.
Break off B.
Next row: Working in A only, K18, slip the next 12 sts in B onto a holder then K the 12 sts of 3rd pocket lining, K to end: 48 sts.
Work a further 22 rows st st.
Break off A, join in D and K 1 row.
Cast off knitwise.

LEFT SLEEVE
Work as given for right sleeve until 10 rows st st in A have been completed.
Work a further 10 rows in A.
Place pocket as follows over page.

More clowning around in the circus ring with these clever and unusual sweaters with their numerous little pockets. The detachable bow ties fasten on to one of the buttons with a loop of thread elastic.

Next row: K18A, 12C, 18A.
Complete pocket as for right sleeve, then work a further 12 rows st st in A.
Break off A, join in D and K 1 row.
Cast off knitwise.

COLLAR

Using 4½mm needles and A, cast on 66 sts.
Work in rib as given for back for 5cm.
Change to 5½mm needles and continue in rib until work measures 8cm.
Break off A, join in B and rib 1 row.
Cast off in rib.

NECKBAND

Join shoulder seams.
With right side facing and using 4½mm needles and A, pick up and K14 sts up right side of front neck, K20 sts from back neck holder, then pick up and K14 sts down left side of front neck: 48 sts.

Work 3 rows in rib as given for back.
Cast off in rib.

BUTTON BORDER

Using 4½mm needles and D, cast on 5 sts.
Work 12 rows in rib as given for back.
Cast off in rib.
Sew into position on left side of neck opening.

BUTTONHOLE BORDER

With right side facing and using 4½mm needles and D, pick up and K5 sts along cast-off sts at neck opening.
Rib 2 rows.
Buttonhole row: Rib 2, yf, K2 tog, K1.
Rib 5 rows.
Work a 2nd buttonhole row, then rib 2 more rows.
Cast off in rib.
Sew border into place, then slipstitch cast-on sts of button border to lower edge of buttonhole border.

These tiny knitted toys are just the right size to fit snuggly into the pockets. Knit them in grey or in bright, contrasting colours.

POCKET TOPS

Lower pocket on front: With right side facing and using 5½mm needles and D, K across sts from holder.
K 2 rows.
Cast off.
Work other pocket tops in the same way using C for the top pocket on front and right sleeve and B for left sleeve.

TO MAKE UP

Fold sleeves in half lengthwise, then placing folds to shoulder seams, sew into place. Join side and sleeve seams. Sew cast-on edge of collar to inside neck edge. Sew on buttons. Press lightly following instructions on ball band.

INSTRUCTIONS FOR BOW TIE

Using 5½mm needles and B, cast on 16 sts.
work 16 rows st st.
Cast off.
Working from chart and using A, Swiss-darn spots onto one half of bow tie.
Fold tie in half and slipstitch edges together.
Using a short length of A, wind yarn tightly round centre of bow tie several times and fasten off securely at back.
Using a small length of elastic, make a loop on back of bow tie to attach to top button on neck of sweater.

INSTRUCTIONS FOR TOYS

All the toys are knitted in double knitting using 4mm needles and are worked in stocking stitch throughout.

CLOWN

Cast on 6 sts in purple and 6 sts in orange.
Keeping colours correct, work 12 rows.
Cast on 5 sts at beg of next 2 rows and work 8 rows.
Cast off 8 sts at beg of next 2 rows.
Change to pink.
Work 1 row.
Cast on 2 sts at beg of next 2 rows.
Work 6 rows.
Cast off 2 sts at beg of next 2 rows.
Work 1 row.
Cast off.
Work a second piece in the same way.

TO MAKE UP

Join 2 pieces together, filling as required. In yellow cast on 6 sts and work 12 rows. Cast off. Fold in half and stitch, then wind yarn tightly round centre to form a bow tie and stitch to neck of clown.
Embroider French knots to form buttons, nose and eyes, then Swiss darn mouth. Using a crochet hook loop short lengths of orange to head to form hair.

ELEPHANT

Using grey cast on 12 sts.
Work 14 rows straight.
Cast on 2 sts at beg of next row.
Work 1 row.
Next row: Cast on 2, work to last 2 sts, work 2 tog.
Work 1 row.
Rep last 2 rows once more.
Next row: Cast on 6 sts; work to last 2 sts, work 2 tog.
Work 1 row.
Dec 1 st at end of next row.
Work 1 row.
Next row: Cast off 8 sts, work to last 2 sts, work 2 tog.
Work 1 row.
Dec 1 st each end of next row.
Work 1 row.
Next row: Cast off 2 sts, work to last 2 sts, work 2 tog.
Cast off.
Make a 2nd piece in the same way, reversing all shapings.
Ear: Using grey, cast on 8 sts.
Work 4 rows.
Dec 1 st each end of next and following alternate row.
Work 1 row.
Cast off.
Work a 2nd piece in the same way.

TO MAKE UP

Join 2 pieces together, filling as required. Embroider French knot to form eye. Join ear pieces together and sew to side of head.

SEAL

Using grey cast on 12 sts.
Work 15 rows.
Dec 1 st at beg of next and every following alternate row until 6 sts remain.
Work 1 row.
Cast off 2 sts at beg of next row.
Work 1 row. Cast off.
Make a 2nd piece in the same way, reversing all shaping.
Flipper: Using grey cast on 2 sts.
Work 2 rows.
Inc 1 st each end of next and following alternate row: 6 sts.
Work 5 rows.
Cast off.
Work a 2nd piece in the same way.

TO MAKE UP

Join 2 pieces together, filling as required. Embroider French knot to form eye. Join flipper pieces together and sew to side of body. Make a small pompon in red (see page 141), and stitch to nose for ball.

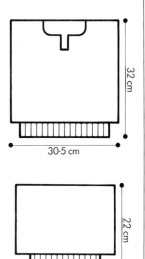

32 cm

30·5 cm

22 cm

28 cm

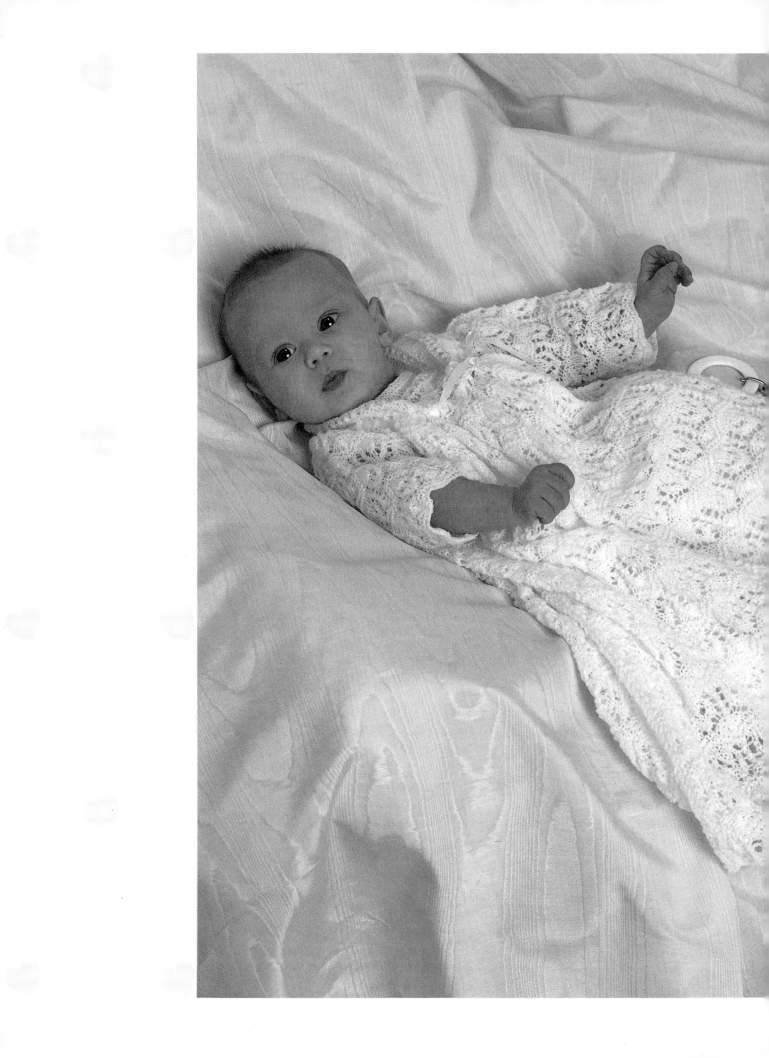

SPECIAL OCCASIONS

Whether it's a christening, a birthday or simply 'Sunday best', special occasions deserve clothes that are a little out of the ordinary. So the designs in this chapter are extra special. There is a delicate christening gown for that first special event, a smart Aran jacket and an adorable party bolero in gorgeous angora. Plus, of course, something for Teddy.

MONDAY'S CHILD

An exquisite design in delicate 2 ply yarn, for that special, special occasion.

MEASUREMENTS
To fit chest 46(48,51) cm [18(19,20) in]
Length to shoulders 56(59,64) cm
Sleeve seam 14(15,17) cm

MATERIALS
3(3,4) × 40 g balls Sirdar Snuggly 2 ply
A pair each of 2¾ mm (No 12), 3¼ mm (No 10) and 3¾ mm (No 9) knitting needles
3 buttons
1.3 metres baby ribbon

TENSION
1 pattern repeat (10 sts) measures 4 cm worked on 3¾ mm needles
10 rows to 5 cm measured over pattern worked on 3¾ mm needles

INSTRUCTIONS

BACK AND FRONT (alike)
Using 3¾ mm needles cast on 153(163,173) sts.
Row 1: Sl 1, K to end.
Rows 2 to 5: As row 1.
Row 6: Sl 1, P1, ✳ yrn, P3, P3 tog, P3, yrn, P1, rep from ✳ to last st, K1.

A christening is a perfect excuse for some delicate lace-effect knitting. The patience such an intricate design requires is well-invested considering the outstanding results it achieves.

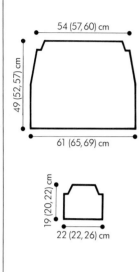

Row 7: Sl 1, K2, ✳ yf, K2, sl 1, K2 tog, psso, K2, yf, K3, rep from ✳ to end.

Row 8: Sl 1, P3, ✳ yrn, P1, P3 tog, P1, yrn, P5, rep from ✳ to last 9 sts, yrn, P1, P3 tog, P1, yrn, P3, K1.

Row 9: Sl 1, K4, ✳ yf, sl 1, K2 tog, psso, yf, K7, rep from ✳ to last 8 sts, yf, sl 1, k2 tog, psso, yf, K5.

Row 10: Sl 1, P2, ✳ K2, P3, rep from ✳ to last 5 sts, K2, P2, K1.

Row 11: Sl 1, K1, ✳ yf, skpo, P1, yon, sl 1, K2 tog, psso, yrn, P1, K2 tog, yf, K1, rep from ✳ to last st, K1.

Row 12: Sl 1, P3, ✳ K1, P3, K1, P5, rep from ✳ to last 9 sts, K1, P3, K1, P3, K1.

Row 13: Sl 1, K2, ✳ yf, skpo, yf, sl 1, K2 tog, psso, yf, K2 tog, yf, K3, rep from ✳ to end.

Row 14: Sl 1, P2, ✳ K1, P5, K1, P3, rep from ✳ to last 10 sts, K1, P5, K1, P2, K1.

Row 15: Sl 1, K2, ✳ P1, K1, yf, sl 1, K2 tog, psso, yf, K1, P1, K3, rep from ✳ to end.

Row 16: Sl 1, P2, ✳ K1, P5, K1, P3, rep from ✳ to last 10 sts, K1, P5, K1, P2, K1.

These 16 rows form the patt.

Continue in patt until work measures 25(27,30) cm from beg, ending with a wrong-side row.

Change to 3¼ mm needles.

Continue in patt until work measures 44(47,52) cm from beg, ending with a wrong-side row.

Shape armholes

Cast off 8 sts at beg of next 2 rows.

Keeping patt correct, dec 1 st each end of next and every following alternate row until 127(137,147) sts remain.

Break off yarn and leave these sts on a spare needle.

SLEEVES

Using 3¼ mm needles cast on 63(63,73) sts.

Work in patt as given for back and front until sleeve measures 14(15,17) cm from beg, ending with a wrong-side row.

Shape top

Cast off 8 sts at beg of next 2 rows.

Keeping patt correct, dec 1 st each end of next and every following alternate row until 37(37,47) sts remain.

Break off yarn and leave these sts on a spare needle.

YOKE

1st and 2nd sizes only

With right side facing slip the first 66(71) sts of back onto a holder, join yarn to next st and using 3¼ mm needles cast on 5 sts, K across these 5 sts then work across remaining 61(66) sts of back as follows: [K2 tog] 8(12) times, [K3 tog] 15(14) times, now work across 37 sts from top of first sleeve as follows: K1, [K2 tog, K2] 9 times, work across 127(137) sts of front as follows: [K3 tog] 13(12) times, [K2 tog] 23(31) times, [K3 tog] 14(13) times, work across

37 sts of second sleeve as follows: [K2, K2 tog] 9 times, K1, then work across 66(71) sts from holder on back as follows: [K3 tog] 15(14) times, [K2 tog] 8(12) times, K5: 162(174) sts.

3rd size only

With right side facing slip the first 76 sts of back onto a holder, join yarn to next st and using 3¼ mm needles cast on 5 sts, K across these 5 sts then work across remaining 71 sts of back as follows: [K2 tog] 16 times, [K3 tog] 13 times, now work across 47 sts from top of first sleeve as follows: [K2 tog] 5 times, [K1, K2 tog] 9 times, [K2 tog] 5 times, work across 147 sts of front as follows: [K3 tog] 11 times, [K2 tog] 39 times, [K3 tog] 12 times, work across 47 sts of second sleeve as follows: [K2 tog] 5 times, [K2 tog, K1] 9 times, [K2 tog] 5 times, then work across 76 sts from holder on back as follows: [K3 tog] 13 times, [K2 tog] 16 times, K5: 186 sts.

All sizes

Row 1: Sl 1, K to end.

Row 2: As row 1.

Row 3: Sl 1, K4, ✳ yrn, P2 tog, rep from ✳ to last 5 sts, K5.

Rows 4 to 6: As row 1.

Row 7: Sl 1, K4, P to last 5 sts, K5.

Row 8: Sl 1, K4, [K1, K2 tog] 7(8,9) times, K31, [K2 tog, K1] 16(18,20) times, K31, [K2 tog, K1] 7(8,9) times, K5: 132(140,148) sts.

Row 9: Sl 1, K4, P to last 5 sts, K5.

Row 10: Sl 1, K to last 3 sts, yf, K2 tog, K1.

Rows 11 and 12: Rep row 1 twice.

Row 13: As row 3.

Rows 14 to 16: Rep row 1 three times.

Row 17: As row 7.

Row 18: Sl 1, K4, [K2 tog, K2] 12(13,14) times, [K2 tog, K3] 4 times, [K2 tog, K2] 13(14,15) times, K2 tog, K5: 102(108,114) sts.

Row 19: Sl 1, K4, P to last 5 sts, K5.

Row 20: Sl 1, K to last 3 sts, yf, K2 tog, K1.

Rows 21 and 22: Rep row 1 twice.

Row 23: As row 3.

Rows 24 to 26: Rep row 1 three times.

Row 27: As row 7.

Row 28: Sl 1, K4, [K2 tog, K3] 18(19,20) times, K2 tog, K5(6,7): 83(88,93) sts.

Row 29: Sl 1, K4, P to last 5 sts, K5.

Change to 2¾ mm needles.

Next row: Sl 1, K to last 3 sts, yf, K2 tog, K1.

Next row: Sl 1, K to end.

Rep the last row 3 times more.

Cast off.

TO MAKE UP

Press lightly following instructions on ball band. Join semi raglan seams up to yoke. Join side and sleeve seams. Sew on buttons. Thread ribbon through first eyelet hole row on yoke, keeping ends at the front. Tie into a bow at front.

SHELL SHAWL

The underside of this shell shawl is almost as pretty as the top. Use it as a shawl, or as a blanket for a crib or Moses basket.

MEASUREMENTS
Approximately 76 cm [30 in] square

MATERIALS
3 × 50 g balls King Cole Superwash 4 ply in each of colours A, B and C
A pair of 3¼ mm (No 10) knitting needles
2·00 mm (No 14) crochet hook

TENSION
38 sts to 15 cm measured over shell patt worked on 3¼ mm needles

The shell effect gives this shawl a slightly raised and gathered texture. The dimensions are for a shawl or crib blanket but it could easily be made larger by increasing the number of stitches worked.

A party jumper (opposite) with special-effects: basically a straightforward round-neck jumper with a back button fastening, that is liberally covered in small bobbles.

SPECIAL ABBREVIATIONS

Shell 6, make a shell as follows: ✻ insert the crochet hook through front of the stitch 5 rows below (the row worked in colour A) the 3rd stitch on left-hand needle and draw through a long loop, slip loop onto right-hand needle, K1, rep from ✻ 5 times more but always insert hook into the same stitch.
Shell 7, finish shell as follows: [P2 tog tbl] 3 times, P1, [P2 tog] 3 times.

SPECIAL NOTE

Always carry colours not in use up side of work, twisting yarns together at side of work on every row to avoid long loops.

INSTRUCTIONS

TO MAKE

Using 3¼ mm needles and A, cast on 192 sts.
K 1 row.
Rows 1 to 6: K with B.
Row 7: With A, K9, [shell 6, K8] 13 times, K1.
Row 8: With A, K2, [K7, shell 7] 13 times, K8.
Rows 9 to 14: K with C.
Row 15: With A, K2, [shell 6, K8] 13 times, shell 6, K2.
Row 16: With A, K2, [shell 7, K7] 13 times, shell 7, K1.
These 16 rows form the patt.
Continue in patt until shawl measures 76 cm from beg, ending with row 8.
Cast off purlwise.

TO FINISH

With right side facing, using the 2·00 mm crochet hook and A, work 2 rows dc evenly along each side of shawl.

GOING DOTTY

Terribly simple but so effective – round-neck jumpers gone dotty!

MEASUREMENTS

Child's jumper
To fit chest 46(51,56) cm [18(20,22) in]
Actual measurements 53(58,63) cm
Length to shoulders 26(30,34) cm
Sleeve seam 18(22,25) cm with cuff turned back
Teddy's jumper
To fit chest 40 cm [16 in]

MATERIALS

Child's jumper
3 × 50 g balls Patons Fairytale 4 ply in main colour A
1 ball same in contrast colour B
Teddy's jumper
1 ball same in main colour A
1 ball same in contrast colour B
For both jumpers
A pair each of 2¾ mm (No 12) and 3¼ mm (No 10) knitting needles
3 buttons.

TENSION

28 sts and 36 rows to 10 cm measured over pattern worked on 3¼ mm needles

SPECIAL ABBREVIATION

MB, Make Bobble using B as follows: K into front, back, front, back and front again of next stitch, then slip the 2nd, 3rd, 4th and 5th stitches from right-hand needle over the first stitch and off the needle.

NOTE

To avoid long loops on back of work, always use a separate length of yarn for each bobble, darning in all ends when making up garment.

INSTRUCTIONS FOR CHILD'S JUMPER

BACK

★ Using 2¾ mm needles and A, cast on 63(69,77) sts.
Rib row 1: K1, ✻ P1, K1, rep from ✻ to end.
Rib row 2: P1, ✻ K1, P1, rep from ✻ to end.
Rep these 2 rows for 4(4,5) cm, ending with rib row 1.
Inc row: Rib 4(2,6), ✻ M1, rib 5(6,6), rep from ✻ to last 4(1,5) sts, M1, rib to end: 75(81,89) sts.
Change to 3¼ mm needles.
Joining on lengths of B as required, work in patt as follows:
Row 1: (Right side) K9(12,2) A, ✻ MB in B, K13 A, rep from ✻ to last 10(13,3) sts, MB in B, K9(12,2) A.
Row 2: P with A.

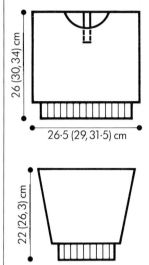

26 (30, 34) cm

26·5 (29, 31·5) cm

22 (26, 3) cm

Row 3: K with A.
Row 4: P with A.
Rows 5 to 8 Rep rows 3 and 4 twice.
Row 9: K2(5,9) A, * MB in B, K13 A, rep from * to last 3(6,10) sts, MB in B, K2(5,9) A.
Row 10: P with A.
Rows 11 to 16: Rep rows 3 and 4 three times.
These 16 rows form the patt. *
Continue in patt until back measures 20(24,28) cm from beg, ending with a wrong-side row.
Divide for back neck opening
Next row: Patt across 35(38,42) sts, turn and leave remaining sts on a spare needle.
Keeping patt correct, continue on these sts until back measures 26(30,34) cm from beg, ending with a wrong-side row.
Next row: Cast off 23(26,29) sts, patt to end.
Break off yarn and leave remaining 12(12,13) sts on a holder.
Return to remaining sts from spare needle.
With right side facing, slip first 5 sts onto a safety-pin, join yarn to remaining sts, patt to end.
Now complete to match first side of neck, reversing all shaping.

FRONT

Work as given for back from * to * .
Continue in patt until front measures 22(26,29) cm from beg, ending with a wrong-side row.
Shape neck
Next row: Patt across 32(34,38) sts, turn and leave remaining sts on a spare needle.
Dec 1 st at neck edge on every row until 23(26,29) sts remain.
Work straight until front measures same as back to shoulders, ending with a wrong-side row.
Cast off.
Return to remaining sts.
With right side facing, slip first 11(13,13) sts onto a holder.
Join on yarn to remaining sts and patt to end.
Now complete to match first side of neck, reversing all shaping.

SLEEVES

Using 2¾ mm needles and A, cast on 37(41,43) sts.
Work 8(8,10) cm in rib as given for back, ending with rib row 1.
Inc row: Rib 5(4,5), * M1, rib 3(3,2), rep from * to last 5(4,4) sts, M1, rib to end: 47(53,61) sts.
Change to 3¼ mm needles.
Work in patt as given for back, increasing and working into patt 1 st each end of 5th and every following 4th(4th,6th) row until there are 67(79,83) sts.
Work straight until sleeve measures 22(26,30) cm, ending with a wrong-side row.
Cast off loosely.

NECKBAND

Join shoulder seams.
With right side facing and using 2¾ mm needles and A, K across 12(12,13) sts from left back neck holder, pick up and K10(11,12) sts down left side of front neck, K across 11(13,13) sts from front neck holder, pick up and K10(11,12) sts up right side of front neck, then K across 12(12,13) sts from right back neck holder: 55(59,63) sts.
Beg rib row 2, work 7 rows in rib.
Cast off in rib.

BUTTON BORDER

Using 2¾ mm needles and A, cast on 7 sts.
Rib row 1: (Right side) K2, * P1, K1, rep from * to last st, K1.
Rib row 2: K1, * P1, K1, rep from * to end.
Rep these 2 rows until border, slightly stretched, fits up left back opening to top of neckband.
Cast off.
Sew on the border and mark the positions for 3 buttons, the top one 1 cm below the top of the border, the lower one 2 cm from cast on edge and the other evenly spaced between.

BUTTONHOLE BORDER

With right side facing and using 2¾ mm needles and A, slip 5 sts from safety-pin onto a needle, then inc into first st, P3, inc into last st: 7 sts.
Now beg with rib row 1, work as given for button band, working buttonholes to correspond with markers as follows:
Buttonhole row: (Right side) Rib 3, yrn, P2 tog, rib to end.

TO MAKE UP

Sew on buttonhole border. Sew lower edge of button border into place behind buttonhole border then sew on the buttons. Sew in the sleeves, then join side and sleeve seams.

INSTRUCTIONS FOR TEDDY'S JUMPER

BACK

** Using 2¾ mm needles and A, cast on 55 sts.
Rib row 1: K1, * P1, K1, rep from * to end.
Rib row 2: P1, * K1, P1, rep from * to end.
Rep these 2 rows for 3 cm, ending with rib row 1.
Inc row: Rib 8, * M1, rib 13, rep from * to last 8 sts, M1, rib to end: 59 sts.
Change to 3¼ mm needles.
Joining on lengths of B as required, work in patt as follows:
Row 1: (Right side) K8A, * MB in B, K13 A, rep from * to last 9 sts, MB in B, K8 A.
Row 2: P with A.
Row 3: K with A.
Row 4: P with A.

Rows 5 to 8: Rep rows 3 and 4 twice.
Row 9: K1 A, ✻ MB in B, K13 A, rep from ✻ to last
2 sts, MB in B, K1 A.
Row 10: P with A.
Rows 11 to 16: Rep rows 3 and 4 three times.
These 16 rows form the patt. ★★
Divide for back neck opening
Next row: Patt across 27 sts, turn and leave
remaining sts on a spare needle.
Keeping patt correct, continue on these sts until back
measures 13 cm from beg, ending with a wrong-side
row.
Next row: Cast off 17 sts, patt to end.
Break off yarn and leave remaining 10 sts on a
holder.
Return to remaining sts.
With right side facing, slip first 5 sts onto a safety-pin,
join yarn to remaining sts, patt to end.
Now complete to match first side of neck, reversing
all shaping.

FRONT

Work as given for back from ★★ to ★★.
Continue in patt until front measures 9 cm from beg,
ending with a wrong-side row.
Shape neck
Next row: Patt across 23 sts, turn and leave
remaining sts on a spare needle.
Dec 1 st at neck edge on every row until 17 sts
remain.
Work straight until front measures same as back to
shoulders, ending with a wrong-side row.
Cast off.
Return to remaining sts.
With right side facing, slip first 13 sts onto a holder,
join on yarn to remaining sts and patt to end.
Now complete to match first side of neck, reversing
all shaping.

SLEEVES

Using 2¾ mm needles and A, cast on 35 sts.
Work 6 cm in rib as given for back, ending with rib
row 1.
Inc row: Rib 4, ✻ M1, rib 3, rep from ✻ to last 4 sts,
M1, rib to end: 45 sts.
Change to 3¼ mm needles.
Work in patt as given for back until sleeve measures
13 cm, ending with a wrong-side row.
Cast off loosely.

NECKBAND

Join shoulder seams.
With right side facing and using 2¾ mm needles and
A, K across 10 sts from left back neck holder, pick up
and K10 sts down left side of front neck, K across
13 sts from front neck holder, pick up and K10 sts up
right side of front neck, then K across 10 sts from
right back neck holder: 53 sts.

Beg rib row 2, work 5 rows in rib.
Cast off in rib.

BUTTON BORDER

Using 2¾ mm needles and A, cast on 7 sts.
Rib row 1: (Right side) K2, ✻ P1, K1, rep from ✻ to
last st, K1.
Rib row 2: K1, ✻ P1, K1, rep from ✻ to end.
Rep these 2 rows until border, slightly stretched, fits
up left back opening to top of neckband.
Cast off.
Sew on the border and mark the positions for 3
buttons, the top one 1 cm below the top of the
border, the lower one 2 cm from cast-on edge and
the other evenly spaced between.

BUTTONHOLE BORDER

With right side facing and using 2¾ mm needles and
A, slip 5 sts from safety-pin onto a needle, then inc
into first st, P3, inc into last st: 7 sts.
Now beg with rib row 1, work as given for button
border working buttonholes to correspond with
markers as follows:
Buttonhole row: (Right side) Rib 3, yrn, P2 tog, rib to
end.

TO MAKE UP

Sew on buttonhole border. Sew lower edge of
button border into place behind buttonhole border
then sew on the buttons. Sew in the sleeves, then join
side and sleeve seams.

"Happy Birthday to you,
Happy Birthday to you,
Happy Birthday dear Teddy,
Happy Birthday to you."

SUNDAY BEST

A very smart double-breasted Aran jacket with a grown-up-looking roll collar. The pattern gives instructions for girls' and boys' buttoning.

MEASUREMENTS

To fit chest 46–51(51–56) cm [18–20(20–22) in]
Actual measurements 64(69) cm
Length to shoulders 33(38) cm
Sleeve seam 21·5(26·5) cm

MATERIALS

8(9) × 50 g balls Aran yarn
A pair each of 3¼ mm (No 10) and 4 mm (No 8) knitting needles
Cable needle
6 buttons

TENSION

20 sts and 26 rows to 10 cm measured over st st worked on 4 mm needles

SPECIAL ABBREVIATIONS

C2F, Cross 2 Front worked as follows: slip next stitch onto cable needle and leave at front of work, P1, then K1 from cable needle.
C2B, Cross 2 Back worked as follows: slip next stitch onto cable needle and leave at back of work, K1, then P1 from cable needle.
MB, Make Bobble as follows: all into next stitch work (K1, P1, K1 and P1), turn and P4, turn and K4, turn and P2 tog twice, then turn and K2 tog.
C4B, Cable 4 Back worked as follows: slip next 2 stitches onto cable needle and leave at back of work, K2, then K2 from cable needle.
C4F, Cable 4 Front worked as follows: slip next 2 stitches onto cable needle and leave at front of work, K2, then K2 from cable needle.

FLOWER STITCH PATTERN

17 sts
Row 1: (Right side) P6, C2B, K1, C2F, P6.
Row 2: K5, C2F, K1, P1, K1, C2B, K5.
Row 3: P4, C2B, P2, K1, P2, C2F, P4.
Row 4: K3, C2F, K3, P1, K3, C2B, K3.
Row 5: P2, C2B, P4, K1, P4, C2F, P2.
Row 6: K2, P1, K5, P1, K5, P1, K2.
Row 7: P2, MB, P5, K1, P5, MB, P2.
Row 8: K8, P1, K8.
Row 9: P8, MB, P8.
Row 10: K17.
Row 11: P17.
Row 12: K17.
Row 13: P17.
Row 14: K8, P1, K8.
These 14 rows form the Flower stitch patt.

HONEYCOMB STITCH PATTERN

16(24) sts
Row 1: (Right side) [C4B, C4F] 2(3) times.
Row 2 and every alternate row: P16(24).
Row 3: K16(24).
Row 5: [C4F, C4B] 2(3) times.
Row 7: K16(24).
Row 8: P16(24).
These 8 rows form the Honeycomb stitch patt.

BACK

Using 3¼ mm needles cast on 63(71) sts.
Rib row 1: K1, * P1, K1, rep from * to end.
Rib row 2: K2, * P1, K1, rep from * to last st, K1.
Rep these 2 rows for 4 cm, ending rib row 2.
Inc row: Rib 8, * inc in next st, rib 11(13), rep from * to last 7 sts, inc in next st, rib to end: 68(76) sts.
Change to 4 mm needles.
Next row: (Wrong side) K1, P3, work [K8, P1, K8] to set flower patt, P3, K2, work P16(24) to set honeycomb patt, K2, P3, work [K8, P1, K8] to set flower patt, P3, K1.
Now work in patt as follows:
Row 1: (Right side) K2, P1, K2, [P6, C2B, K1, C2F, P6] for first row of flower patt, K1, P1, K1, P2, [C4B, C4F] 2(3) times for first row of honeycomb patt, P2, K1, P1, K1, [P6, C2B, K1, C2F, P6] for first row of flower patt, K1, P1, K2.
Row 2: K1, P3, [K5, C2F, K1, P1, K1, C2B, K5] for second row of flower patt, P3, K2, P16(24) for second row of honeycomb patt, K2, P3, [K5, C2F, K1, P1, K1, C2B, K5] for second row of flower patt, P3, K1.
These 2 rows set position for flower and honeycomb patts.
Repeating rows 1 and 2 for borders in between pattern panels, continue in patt until back measures approximately 33(38) cm from beg, ending with row 14 of flower patt.
Next row: Cast off 25 sts, patt until there are 18(26) sts on the needle, then cast off remaining 25 sts.

FRONTS (both alike)

Using 3¼ mm needles cast on 23 sts.
Work 4 cm in rib as given for back, ending rib row 1, increasing 1 st each end of last row: 25 sts.
Change to 4 mm needles.
Next row: (Wrong side) K1, P3, work [K8, P1, K8] to set flower patt, P3, K1.
Work in patt as follows:
Row 1: (Right side) K2, P1, K1, [P6, C2B, K1, C2F, P6] for flower patt, K1, P1, K2.
Continue in patt as set until front measures the same as back to shoulders, ending with row 14 of the flower patt.
Cast off.

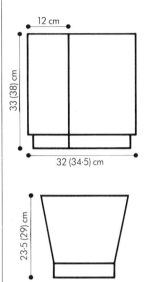

12 cm

33 (38) cm

32 (34·5) cm

23·5 (29) cm

SLEEVES

Using 3¼ mm needles cast on 37 sts.
Work 4(5) cm in rib as given for back ending rib row 2.
Inc row: Rib 6, ✳ inc in next st, rib 3, rep from ✳ to last 7 sts, inc in next st, rib to end: 44 sts.
Change to 4 mm needles.
Next row: (Wrong side) K5, P3, K2, P24 to set honeycomb patt, K2, P3, K5.
Work in patt as follows:
Row 1: (Right side) K1, P4, K1, P1, K1, P2, [C4B, C4F] 3 times for honeycomb patt, P2, K1, P1, K1, P4, K1.
Row 2: K5, P3, K2, P24 for honeycomb patt, K2, P3, K5.
These 2 rows set patt, continue in patt increasing and working into rev st st 1 st each end of 5th and every following 4th row until there are 54(64) sts.
Work straight until sleeve measures approximately 21·5(26·5) cm from beg with cuff turned back, ending with a wrong-side row.
Cast off.

COLLAR

Button band (left for a girl or right for a boy)
Join shoulder seams.
With right side facing and using 3¼ mm needles, pick up and K85(99) sts along front edge and K13 sts from back neck sts on holder (leaving remaining sts for buttonhole band): 98(112) sts.
Work 10(12·5) cm in K1, P1 rib.
Cast off in rib.
Mark positions for 3 pairs of buttons, the first pair 3 cm from lower edge and 2·5 cm in from each side, then the other 2 pairs at 7·5 cm intervals.
Buttonhole band
Work as given for button band, working buttonholes when rib measures 2·5 cm and 7·5(10) cm to correspond with markers as follows:
Buttonhole row: (Right side) Rib to position for first buttonhole, ending with a P1, ✳ K2 tog, yrn, rib to next position for buttonhole, rep from ✳ once more, K2 tog, yrn, rib to end.

TO MAKE UP

Join collar at centre back neck. Fold sleeves in half lengthwise, then placing fold at top of sleeves to shoulder seams, sew in sleeves. Join side and sleeve seams. Sew on buttons.

PARTY PIECE

A traditional party piece – beautifully soft angora bolero knitted in one.

MEASUREMENTS

To fit chest 46–51(51–56) cm [18–20(20–22) in]
Actual measurements 50(56) cm
Length to shoulders 18·5(21) cm
Sleeve seam 8·5 cm

MATERIALS

2(3) × 20 g balls of Jaeger Angora Spun
A pair of 3¾ mm (No 9) knitting needles

TENSION

25 sts and 33 rows to 10 cm measured over st st worked on 3¾ mm needles

INSTRUCTIONS

RIGHT FRONT

Using 3¾ mm needles cast on 17(21) sts.
Shape front edge and work moss st border as follows:

Row 1: Inc into first st, [P1, K1] to end.
Row 2: [K1, P1] to last 2 sts, inc into next st, K1.
Rows 3 to 8: Rep rows 1 and 2 three times: 25(29) sts.
Row 9: Work in moss st over first 7 sts, inc into next st, K to end.
Row 10: K1, P to last 7 sts, moss st 7.
Rep rows 9 and 10 until there are 31(35) sts.
Keeping moss st border correct, continue in patt until front measures 9(11·5) cm from beg, ending with a right-side row.

Shape for sleeve

Row 1: Cast on 7 sts, K1, P to last 7 sts, moss st 7: 38(42) sts.

Row 2: Moss st 7, K to end.
Rows 3 and 4: As rows 1 and 2: 45(49) sts.
Row 5: Cast on 7 sts, then moss st 7, P to last 7 sts, moss st 7: 52(56) sts.
Row 6: Moss st 7, K to last 7 sts, moss st 7.

Shape neck

Next row: Moss st 7, P to last 10 sts, P2 tog, P1, moss st 7.
Keeping moss st borders correct, work 3 rows straight.
Rep the last 4 rows until 45(49) sts remain.
Work straight until sleeve border measures 8 cm from beg of shaping.
Place a marker at each end of last row to denote shoulder line.
Work straight in patt for a further 2·5 cm, ending with a wrong-side row.
Break off yarn.
Leave sts on a spare needle.

Soft fluffy yarn guarantees that this classic bolero will continue to be a firm party favourite for years to come. An essential item in every well-dressed little girl's wardrobe!

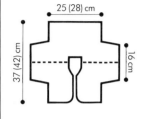

25 (28) cm

37 (42) cm

16 cm

This little waistcoat with its two front pockets is another classic design employing traditional techniques. There are instructions for both boys' and girls' buttoning.

LEFT FRONT

Using 3¾ mm needles cast on 17(21) sts.
Shape front edge and work moss st border as follows:
Row 1: [K1, P1] to last 3 sts, K1, P twice into next st, K1.
Row 2: Inc into first st, [K1, P1] to last st, K1.
Rows 3 to 8: Rep rows 1 and 2 three times: 25(29) sts.
Row 9: K to last 9 sts, inc into next st, K1, work in moss st to end.
Row 10: Moss st 7, P to last st, K1.
Rep rows 9 and 10 until there are 31(35) sts.
Keeping moss st border correct, continue in patt until front measures 9(11·5) cm from beg, ending with a wrong-side row.
Shape for sleeve
Row 1: Cast on 7 sts, K to last 7 sts, moss st 7: 38(42) sts.
Row 2: Moss st 7, P to last st, K1.
Rows 3 and 4: As rows 1 and 2: 45(49) sts.
Row 5: Cast on 7 sts, then moss st 7, K to last 7 sts, moss st 7: 52(56) sts.
Row 6: Moss st 7, P to last 7 sts, moss st 7.
Shape neck
Next row: Moss st 7, K to last 10 sts, K2 tog, K1, moss st 7.
Keeping moss st borders correct, work 3 rows straight.
Rep the last 4 rows until 45(49) sts remain.
Work straight until sleeve border measures 8 cm from beg of shaping.
Place a marker at each end of last row to denote shoulder line.
Work straight in patt for a further 2·5 cm, ending with a wrong-side row.
Back
Next row: Patt across left front to last st, sl 1, turn and cast on 15 sts for back neck, turn and with right side facing, patt across sts of right front from spare needle: 105(113) sts.
Next row: Moss st 7, P31(35), moss st 29, P31(35), moss st 7.
Keeping moss st correct, work 6 more rows.
Next row: Moss st 7, K to last 7 sts, moss st 7.
Next row: Moss st 7, P to last 7 sts, moss st 7.
Rep these 2 rows until sleeve borders measure 16 cm from beg, ending with a wrong-side row.
Shape sleeves
Cast off 7 sts at beg of next 6 rows: 63(71) sts.
Continuing in st st, work straight until back measures same as fronts from underarm to beg of moss st border, ending with P row.
Next row: K1, [P1, K1] to end.
Rep this row 7 times more. Cast off purlwise.

TO MAKE UP

Join side and sleeve seams. Press lightly following instructions on ball band.

BIRTHDAY BOY

A smart waistcoat with a clever cable rib.

MEASUREMENTS
To fit chest 51–56 cm [20–22 in]
Actual measurements 60 cm
Length to shoulders 33 cm

MATERIALS
3 × 50 g balls King Cole Superwash DK
A pair each of 3¼ mm (No 10) and 4 mm (No 8) knitting needles
Cable needle
Set of four 3¼ mm (No 10) double-pointed needles or a circular needle

TENSION
24 sts and 32 rows to 10 cm measured over st st worked on 4 mm needles

SPECIAL ABBREVIATION
C4B, Cable 4 Back worked as follows: slip next 2 sts onto a cable needle and leave at back of work, K2, then K2 from cable needle.

INSTRUCTIONS

POCKET LININGS (make 2)
Using 3¼ mm needles cast on 20 sts.
Work 5 cm st st, ending with a P row.
Break off yarn and leave sts on a spare needle.

BACK AND FRONTS
(Worked in one piece to armholes)
Using 3¼ mm needles cast on 136 sts.
Work in cable rib as follows:
Row 1: K1, ✲ P2, K4, rep from ✲ to last 3 sts, P2, K1.
Row 2 and every alternate row: K3, ✲ P4, K2, rep from ✲ to last st, K1.
Row 3: As row 1.
Row 5: K1, ✲ P2, C4B, rep from ✲ to last 3 sts, P2, K1.
Row 7: As row 1.
Row 9: As row 1.
Row 11: As row 5.
Row 13: As row 1.
Row 14: (Inc row) K3, P4, K2 to form the 9 border sts, K3, [inc in next st, K7] 4 times, inc into next st, K4, K2, P4, K2, K2 tog, K18, K2 tog, K2, P4, K2, K4, [inc into next st, K7] 4 times, inc into next st, K3, K2, P4, K3: 144 sts.
Change to 4 mm needles.
Now work in patt as follows:
Row 1: (Right side) K1, P2, K4, P2 for border, P20 for pocket, [K1, P1] 12 times, K1 to form moss st, P2, K4, P2 for cable, P20 for patt panel, P2, K4, P2 for cable,

[K1, P1] 12 times, K1 for moss st, P20 for pocket, P2, K4, P2, K1 for border.

Row 2: K3, P4, K2 for border, [P3 tog, work (K1, P1 and K1) all into next st] 5 times for pocket, [K1, P1] 12 times, K1 for moss st, K2, P4, K2 for cable, [P3 tog, work (K1, P1 and K1) all into next st] 5 times for patt panel, K2, P4, K2 for cable, [K1, P1] 12 times, K1 for moss st, [P3 tog, work (K1, P1 and K1) all into next st] 5 times for pocket, K2, P4, K3 for border.

Row 3: K1, P2, C4B, P2 for border, P20 for pocket, moss st 25, P2, C4B, P2 for cable, P20 for patt panel, P2, C4B, P2 for cable, moss st 25, P20 for pocket, P2, C4B, P2, K1 for border.

Row 4: K3, P4, K2 for border, [work (K1, P1 and K1) all into next st, P3 tog] 5 times for pocket, moss st 25, cable 8, [work (K1, P1 and K1) all into next st, P3 tog] 5 times for patt panel, cable 8, moss st 25, [work (K1, P1 and K1) all into next st, P3 tog] 5 times for pocket, K2, P4, K3 for border.

These 4 rows form the bobble patt over pockets and centre back panel.

Continue in patt as set, working cable twists (C4B) every 6 rows until work measures approximately 9 cm from beg, ending with a wrong-side row.

Next row: Patt across 9 border sts, slip next 20 sts onto a holder then [K1, P1] 10 times across one pocket lining from spare needle, patt across 25 sts of moss st panel, work across cable and patt panels, then patt across 25 sts of moss st panel, slip next 20 sts onto a holder and [K1, P1] 10 times across second pocket lining from spare needle, work across 9 border sts to end: 144 sts.

Next row: Patt across 9 border sts, moss st across next 45 sts, cable 8, patt across centre panel, cable 8, moss st across next 45 sts, work across 9 border sts to end.

Keeping patt correct as now set, continue in patt until work measures 19 cm from beg, ending with a wrong-side row.

Divide for armholes

Next row: Patt across 36 sts, turn and leave remaining sts on a spare needle.

Next row: Cast off 3 sts, patt to end.

Next row: Patt 9, work 2 tog, patt to last 2 sts, work 2 tog.

Next row: Work 2 tog, patt to end.

Rep these 2 rows until 24 sts remain.

Next row: Patt 9, work 2 tog, patt to last 2 sts, work 2 tog.

Next row: Patt to end.

Rep these 2 rows until 16 sts remain.

Keeping armhole edge straight, continue to dec within the 9 st border on next and every following alternate row until 10 sts remain.

Work straight until front measures 33 cm from beg, ending with a wrong-side row.

Cast off.

Return to remaining sts.

With right side facing, join on yarn and patt across first 72 sts.

Cast off 3 sts at beg of next 2 rows.

Dec 1 st each end of following 7 rows, then dec 1 st each end of every following alternate row until 46 sts remain.

Work straight until back measures 2 rows less than right front, ending with a wrong-side row.

Shape shoulders

Cast off 10 sts at beg of next 2 rows.

Break off yarn and leave remaining 26 sts on a holder.

Return to remaining sts.

With right side facing, rejoin yarn and cast off first 3 sts, patt to end.

Patt 1 row.

Next row: Work 2 tog, patt to last 11 sts, work 2 tog, patt to end.

Next row: Patt to last 2 sts, work 2 tog.

Rep these 2 rows until 24 sts remain.

Next row: Work 2 tog, patt to last 11 sts, work 2 tog, patt to end.

Next row: Patt to end.

Rep these 2 rows until 16 sts remain.

Now complete to match right front.

NECKBAND

Join shoulder seams.

With right side facing and using 3 mm needles, pick up and K106 sts evenly up right front to shoulder, P across 26 sts from back neck holder, then pick up and K106 sts evenly down left front: 238 sts.

Row 1: K to end.

Row 2: K1, ✶ P2, C4B, rep from ✶ to last 3 sts, P2, K1.

Row 3: K3, ✶ P4, K2, rep from ✶ to last st, K1.

Boy's waistcoat

Row 4: K1, [P2, K4] 29 times, [P2, K2 tog, yrn, K2 tog tbl] 10 times, P2, K1.

Row 5: K3, [P1, P twice into next loop, P1, K2] 10 times, [P4, K2] 29 times, K1.

Girl's waistcoat

Row 4: K1, [P2, K2 tog, yrn, K2 tog tbl] 10 times, [P2, K4] 29 times, P2, K1.

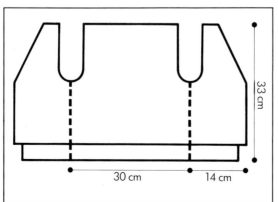

30 cm   14 cm   33 cm

Row 5: K3, [P4, K2] 29 times, [P1, P twice into next loop, P1, K2] 10 times, K1.
Boy's or Girl's waistcoat
Row 6: K1, ✳ P2, K4, rep from ✳ to last 3 sts, P2, K1.
Rows 7 and 8: As rows 3 and 2.
Cast off knitwise.

ARMBANDS

With right side facing, using set of 4 double-pointed or circular needle and beg at underarm, pick up and K78 sts evenly round armhole.
Round 1: P to end.
Round 2: [K4, P2] to end.
Round 3: [C4B, P2] to end.
Rounds 4 to 8: Rep round 2 five times.
Round 9: As round 3.
Cast off knitwise.

POCKET TOPS

With right side facing and using 3¼ mm needles work across 20 sts from holder as follows:
Row 1: P2, [P twice into next st, P2] 6 times: 26 sts.
Row 2: K2, ✳ P4, K2, rep from ✳ to end.
Row 3: P2, ✳ C4B, P2, rep from ✳ to end.
Row 4: K2, ✳ P4, K2, rep from ✳ to end.
Row 5: P2, ✳ K4, P2, rep from ✳ to end.
Rows 6 and 7: As rows 4 and 5.
Row 8: As row 4.
Row 9: As row 3.
Cast off purlwise.

TO MAKE UP

Sew on buttons where required, using eyelet holes in cables as buttonholes.
Sew down ends of pocket tops.

DICKY BOW

A cute little bow tie that fastens at the back.

MATERIALS

Small amount of Chenille (approximately DK thickness)
A pair of 2¾ mm (No 12) knitting needles
3·00 mm crochet hook

INSTRUCTIONS

TO MAKE

Cast on 1 st.
Row 1: K into front and back of st: 2 sts.
Row 2: P into front and back of first st, P1: 3 sts.
Continue in st st until work measures 7·5 cm from beg.
Shape centre of bow
Dec 1 st at beg of next 2 rows: 1 st.
Now inc 1 st at beg of next 2 rows: 3 sts.
Continue in st st until work measures 15 cm from beg.
Shape end
Dec 1 st at beg of next 2 rows: 1 st.
Break off yarn and fasten off.

CENTRE BAND

Cast on 2 sts.
Beg K row work in st st for 5 cm, ending P row.
Cast off.

TO MAKE UP

Using crochet hook, crochet a chain approximately 61 cm long. Fold bow by placing cast-on and cast-off points to centre back and stitch to secure. Fold band over centre of bow and stitch at back. Knot crocheted chain over back of band and secure to back of bow with small stitches.

This smart chenille bow tie makes a special-occasion outfit really special. The bow is stitched together to make it sturdy and fastens at the back of the neck with a length of crocheted chain.

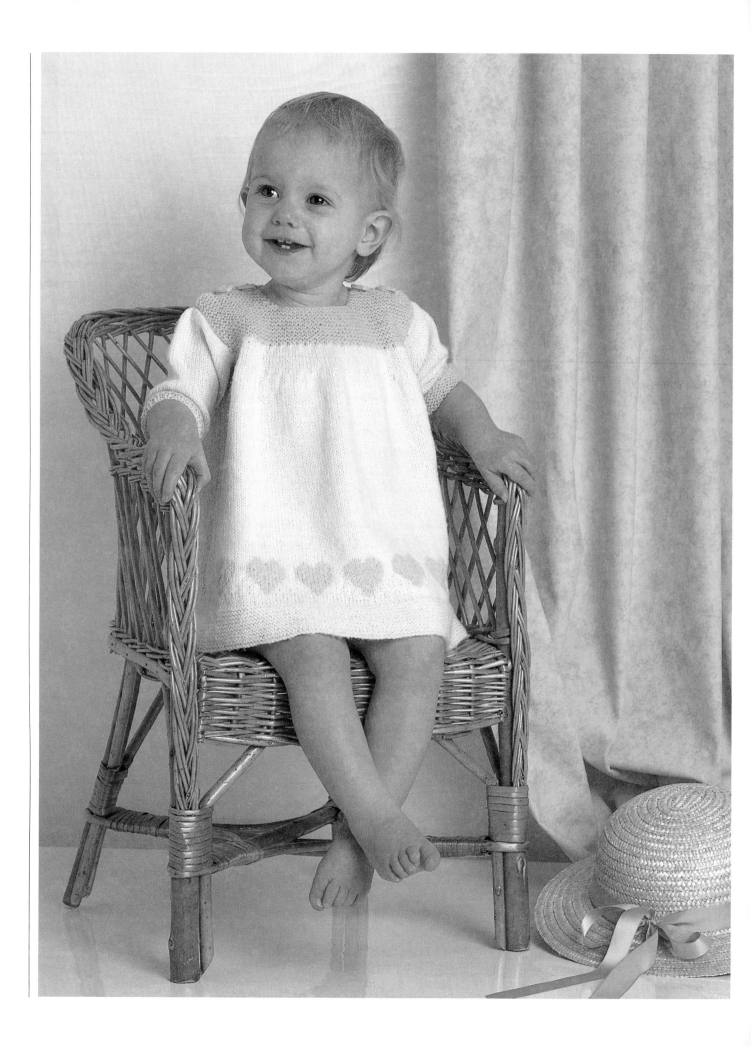

QUEEN OF HEARTS

Peach hearts and garter stitch make a simple little dress good enough for a special occasion!

MEASUREMENTS

To fit chest 41—46(46—51) cm [16—18(18—20) in]
Length to shoulders 34·5(40) cm
Sleeve seam 12·5(18) cm

MATERIALS

2(3) × 50 g balls Schaffhauser 3 ply Lambswool in main colour A
1 ball same in contrast colour B
A pair each of 3 mm (No 11) and 3¼ mm (No 10) knitting needles; 4 buttons

TENSION

32 sts and 40 rows to 10 cm measured over st st worked on 3¼ mm needles

INSTRUCTIONS

FRONT

★ Using 3 mm needles and A, cast on 129 sts.
K 20 rows.
Change to 3¼ mm needles.
Beg K row, work 4 rows st st.
Work in patt, placing heart motifs from chart as follows:
Row 1: K8A, ✳ 1B, 13 A, rep from ✳ to last 9 sts, K1B, 8A.
Row 2: P7A, ✳ 3B, 11A, rep from ✳ to last 10 sts, P3B, 7A.
Continue in patt from chart until row 12 has been completed.
Using A only, continue in st st, until front measures 25·5(28) cm from beg, ending with a P row.
Shape armholes
Next row: Cast off 3 sts, then [K2, K2, tog] 30 times, K to end.
Next row: Cast off 3 sts, P to end: 93 sts.
Dec 1 st each end of next and every following alternate row until 85 sts remain, ending with a P row.

Break off A and join on B.
Next row: ✳ K1, K2 tog, rep from ✳ to last st, K1: 57 sts. ★
K 20(30) rows.
Shape neck
Next row: (Wrong side) K19, cast off 19, K to end.
Working on first set of sts, K 13(17) rows.
Cast off.
Return to remaining sts.
Join on B and complete to match first side of neck.

BACK

Work as given for front from ★ to ★.
K 34(48) rows.
Cast off.

SLEEVES

Using 3¼ mm needles and B, cast on 33(39) sts.
K 14 rows.
Break off B and join on A.
Work in rib as follows:
Rib row 1: K2, ✳ P1, K1, rep from ✳ to last st, K1.
Rib row 2: K1, ✳ P1, K1, rep from ✳ to end.
Rep these 2 rows 4 times more.
Inc row: ✳ K3, M1, rep from ✳ to last 3 sts, K3: 43(51) sts.
Beg with a P row, work 3 rows st st.
Continuing in st st, inc 1 st each end of next and every following 4th row until there are 61(77) sts.
Work straight until sleeve measures 15(20·5) cm from beg, ending with a P row.
Shape top
Cast off 3 sts at beg of next 2 rows.
Dec 1 st each end of next and every following alternate row until 47(63) sts remain, ending with a P row.
Cast off.

TO MAKE UP

Join shoulder seams for about 2 cm on each shoulder. Make 2 Buttonloops on each front shoulder. Sew buttons to back shoulders to correspond with buttonloops. Sew in sleeves. Join side and sleeve seams. Press lightly following instructions on ball band.

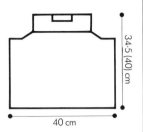

40 cm
34·5 (40) cm

19 (24) cm
17·5 (23) cm

Knitted in delicate 3 ply, this pretty little hearts dress has three-quarter length sleeves with turn-back cuffs. The square neck has shoulder fastenings of buttons and button loops.

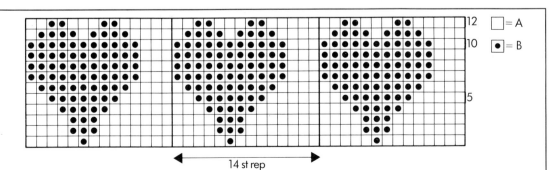

12
10
5
□ = A
• = B

14 st rep

SEASIDE SPECIAL

Summer knitwear for babies and toddlers needs to be varied – cool enough for scorching weather, practical enough to withstand beach antics and frequent washing, and warm enough for the odd blustery day. Here, among other things, are cool white cotton knits, a pretty sundress and a traditional Guernsey for would-be fishermen ... and not forgetting outfits for Teddy, too!

SHIP AHOY!

A sleeveless cotton top which can either be worn alone or over a T-shirt.

MEASUREMENTS
To fit chest 51(56) cm [20(22) in]
Actual measurements 56(61) cm
Length to shoulders 28(30·5) cm

MATERIALS
2 × 50 g balls Phildar Perle No 5 or Fil d'Ecosse in main colour A
1 ball same in each of contrast colours B and C
A pair each of 2¼ mm (No 13) and 2¾ mm (No 12) knitting needles

TENSION
32 sts and 44 rows to 10 cm measured over st st worked on 2¾ mm needles

INSTRUCTIONS

BACK
★ Using 2¼ mm needles and B, cast on 91(99) sts.
Rib row 1: K1, ☆ P1, K1, rep from ☆ to end.
Rib row 2: K2, ☆ P1, K1, rep from ☆ to last st, K1.
Rep these 2 rows for 4 cm, ending rib row 2.
Change to 2¾ mm needles.
Beg K row, work 4 rows st st.
Work motifs from chart as follows on next page:

A little nautical nonsense with these charming seaside tops. They are knitted in fine cotton which makes them light enough by themselves for a heatwave, or suitable to wear over a T-shirt. And, surprise, surprise, the boats re-appear on the back! See over page for the back view.

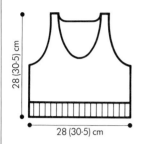

28 (30·5) cm

28 (30·5) cm

1st size only
Row 1: K1A, ✩ 4B, 2A, rep from ✩ to end.
Row 2: P3A, ✩ 2B, 4A, rep from ✩ to last 4 sts, K2B, 2A.
2nd size only
Row 1: K3B, ✩ 2A, 4B, rep from ✩ to end.
Row 2: P1A, ✩ 2B, 4A, rep from ✩ to last 2 sts, P2B.
Break off B.
Work 2 rows A.
Now continuing from chart, work as follows:
Row 5: K18(22)A, 12C, 12A, 12C, 12A, 12C, 13(17)A.
Row 6: P12(16)A, 20C, 4A, 20C, 4A, 20C, 11(15)A.
Continue in this way working from chart until row 34 has been completed.
Working in A only, continue in st st until back measures 14(16.5) cm from beg, ending with a P row.
Shape armholes
Next row: K5 and slip these sts onto a safety pin, K to end.
Next row: P5 and slip these sts onto a safety pin, P to end: 81(89) sts.
Dec 1 st each end of every row to 59(67) sts, then every following alternate row until 51(59) sts remain. ★
Work straight until back measures 26(28·5) cm from beg, ending with a P row.
Shape neck
Next row: K16(20), turn and leave remaining sts on a spare needle.
Dec 1 st at neck edge on every row until 8(12) sts remain.
Cast off.
Return to sts on spare needle.
With right side facing, slip first 19 sts onto a holder, join yarn to next st and complete to match first side of neck.

FRONT
Work as given for back from ★ to ★.
Shape neck
Next row: K20(24), turn and leave remaining sts on a spare needle.
Dec 1 st at neck edge on next and every following alternate row until 8(12) sts remain.
Work straight until front measures same as back to shoulders.
Return to sts on spare needle.
With right side facing, slip first 11 sts onto a holder, join yarn to next st and complete 2nd side of neck to match first.

NECKBAND
Join right shoulder seam.
With right side facing, 2¼ mm needles and A, pick up and K36 sts down left side of front neck, K across 11 sts from holder, pick up and K35 sts up right side of neck and 7 sts down right back neck, K across 19 sts from holder, then pick up and K7 sts up left back neck: 115 sts.
Beg rib row 2, work 7 rows rib.
Cast off knitwise.

ARMHOLE BORDERS
Join left shoulder and neckband seam.
With right side facing, 2¼ mm needles and A, pick up and K115 sts evenly round armhole, including the 5 sts at each end on safety pins.
Beg rib row 2, work 7 rows rib.
Cast off knitwise.

TO MAKE UP
Join side and armhole border seams.
Press according to instructions on ball band.

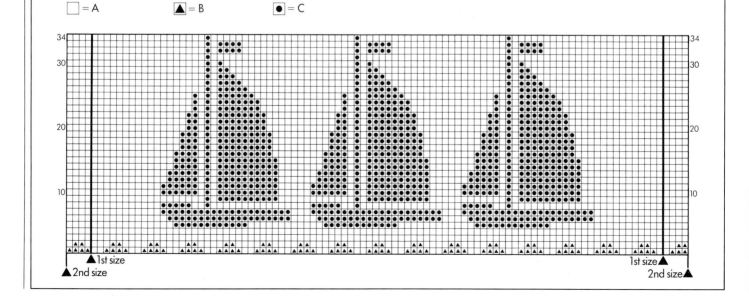

☐ = A   ▲ = B   ● = C

1st size   2nd size

"I saw a ship a-sailing,
A-sailing on the sea,
And oh but it was laden
With pretty things for thee.

There were comfits in the
    cabin,
And apples in the hold;
The sails were made of silk,
And the masts were all of
    gold.

The four-and-twenty sailors,
That stood between the decks,
Were four-and-twenty white
    mice
With chains about their necks.

The captain was a duck
With a pack upon his back,
And when the ship began to
    move,
The captain said Quack!
    Quack!"

SAILOR STRIPES

A two-piece sailor suit consisting of square-necked T-shirt and Bermuda shorts.

MEASUREMENTS
Child's T-shirt
To fit chest 46(51,56) cm [18(20,22) in]
Actual measurements 51(56,61) cm
Length to shoulders 25·5(28,30·5) cm
Sleeve seam 7·5 cm
Child's shorts
To fit waist 51 to 56 cm [20 to 22 in]
Waist to crutch 20·5 cm
Inside leg 15·5 cm (adjustable)
Teddy's T-shirt and shorts
To fit chest 38 cm [15 in]
Height 48 cm [19 in]

MATERIALS
Child's T-shirt
2 × 50 g balls Phildar Perle No 5 or Fil d'Ecosse in main colour A
1 ball same in contrast colour B
Child's shorts
2 balls same in main colour A
1 ball same in contrast colour B
Waist length of elastic
Teddy's T-shirt
1 ball same in main colour A
1 ball same in contrast colour B
2·00 mm (No 14) crochet hook
One button
Teddy's shorts
1 ball same in main colour A
1 ball same in contrast colour B
Waist length of elastic
For all garments
A pair each of 2¼ mm (No 13) and 2¾ mm (No 12) knitting needles
A set of four double-pointed 2¼ mm (No 13) knitting needles or one circular 2¼ mm (No 13) needle

TENSION
32 sts and 44 rows to 10 cm measured over st st worked on 2¾ mm needles

INSTRUCTIONS FOR CHILD'S T-SHIRT

BACK
★ Using 2¼ mm needles and A, cast on 83(91, 99) sts.
Rib row 1: K1, ✻ P1, K1, rep from ✻ to end.
Rib row 2: P1, ✻ K1, P1, rep from ✻ to end.
Rep these 2 rows for 4 cm, ending rib row 2.
Change to 2¾ mm needles.
Proceeding in st st, work in stripes of 2 rows A and 2

rows B until back measures 14(16·5,19) cm from beg, ending with a P row.
Place a marker at each end of last row to denote beg of armhole. ★
Continue in st st stripes until back measures 23(25·5,28)cm from beg, ending with a P row.
Shape back neck
Keeping stripe patt correct, K22(25,29) then turn and leave remaining sts on a spare needle.
Work straight for a further 2·5 cm, ending with a P row in A. Cast off.
Return to sts on spare needle.
With right side facing, slip first 41 sts onto a holder, then complete second side to match first.

FRONT
Work as given for back from ★ to ★ .
Continue in st st stripes until front measures 18(20·5,23) cm from beg, ending with a P row.
Shape front neck
Keeping stripe patt correct, K22(25,29) then turn and leave remaining sts on a spare needle.
Work straight until front measures same as back to shoulders, ending with a P row. Cast off.
Return to sts on spare needle.
With right side facing, slip first 41 sts onto a holder, then complete second side to match first.

SLEEVES
Join shoulder seams.
With right side facing and using 2¾ mm needles and A, pick up and K75 sts between armhole markers.
P 1 row.
Beg with B, work in 2 row st st stripes until sleeve measures 5·5 cm from beg, ending with a P row.
Change to 2¼ mm needles.
Beg rib row 2 and using A, work 7 rows rib.
Cast off knitwise.

NECK
With right side facing, set of four double pointed needles or circular needle and A, join yarn at neck on left shoulder and pick up and K24 sts down left front neck, K across 41 sts from holder, pick up and K24 sts up right side of front neck, 9 sts down right back neck, K across 41 sts from holder, then pick up and K9 sts up left back neck: 148 sts.
Working in rounds, K 1 round.
Now shape neck as follows:
Round 1: (Dec round) [K1, P1] 10 times, K1, P2 tog, K corner st, P2 tog, [K1, P1] 18 times, K1, P2 tog, K corner st, P2 tog, [K1, P1] 13 times, K1, P2 tog, K corner st, P2 tog, [K1, P1] 18 times, K1, P2 tog, K corner st, P2 tog, [K1, P1] 3 times.
Round 2: Rib to end.
Work 5 more rounds in rib, working P2 tog either side of corner sts on next and every following alternate row. Cast off purlwise.

Delightful little cotton outfits – reminiscent of Victorian bathing suits – that are simple, practical and easy to wear. Substitute navy blue or red in place of pale blue for a very different effect.

Dressing Teddy in his version of 'Sailor Stripes' is child's play! His T-shirt has a single button at the back, making it easy to put on.

TO MAKE UP

Join side and sleeve seams. Press following instructions on the ball band.

INSTRUCTIONS FOR CHILD'S SHORTS

RIGHT LEG

★ Using 2¼ mm needles and A, cast on 85 sts.
Beg with a K row, work 10 rows st st.
Change to 2¾ mm needles.
Work a further 10 rows st st.
Fold work in half to wrong side and make hem as follows:
Next row: K1, pick up first loop from cast-on edge and K tog with next st on left-hand needle, ✿ pick up next loop from cast-on edge and K tog with next st on left-hand needle, rep from ✿ to end.
P 1 row.
Now working in stripes of 2 rows B and 2 rows A, continue straight in st st until leg measures 10 cm from lower edge (or length required), ending with a P row.
Shape crutch
Inc 1 st each end of next and every following 3rd row until there are 101 sts.
Work 2 rows straight, so ending P row. ★
Shape back
Dec 1 st at end of next and every following 6th row until 88 sts remain.

Work 2 rows straight, so ending K row.
Breaking off yarn and rejoining as necessary, continue as follows:
Row 1: P to last 12 sts, turn.
Row 2 and every alternate row: K to end.
Row 3: P to last 20 sts, turn.
Row 5: P to last 28 sts, turn.
Row 7: P to last 36 sts, turn.
Row 9: P across all 88 sts.
Break off yarn and leave sts on a spare needle.

LEFT LEG

Work as given for right leg from ★ to ★.
Shape back
Dec 1 st at beg of next and every following 6th row until 88 sts remain, so ending K row. P 1 row.
Now continue as follows:
Row 1: K to last 12 sts, turn.
Row 2 and every alternate row: P to end.
Row 3: K to last 20 sts, turn.
Row 5: K to last 28 sts, turn.
Row 7: K to last 36 sts, turn.
Row 9: K across all 88 sts.
Row 10: P to end.
Do not break off yarn.

WAISTBAND

Next row: Using 2¼ mm needles and A, K across the first 87 sts of left leg, then working across sts of right

leg, K tog the last st of left leg with first st of right leg, K across remaining 87 sts: 175 sts.
Beg P row, work a further 20 rows st st.
Cast off.

TO MAKE UP
Join inside leg seams. Join front and back seams. Fold waistband in half to wrong side and slipstitch into place, leaving an opening for elastic. Thread elastic into casing and secure. Press following instructions on the ball band.

INSTRUCTIONS FOR TEDDY'S T-SHIRT

BACK
★ Using 2¼ mm needles and A, cast on 65 sts.
Rep 6 rows in rib as given for baby's T-shirt, inc 1 st at end of last row: 66 sts.
Change to 2¾ mm needles.
Working in stripes of 2 rows B and 2 rows A, continue in st st until back measures 9 cm from beg, ending with a P row
Place a marker at each end of last row to denote beg of armholes. ★
Divide for back opening
Next row: K33, turn and leave remaining sts on a spare needle.
Continue in st st stripes on these sts until back measures 16·5 cm from beg, ending with a P row.
Shape neck
Next row: K17, turn and leave remaining sts on a holder.
Continue on these sts until work measures 19 cm from beg, ending with a P row.
Cast off.
Return to sts on spare needle and complete to match first side, reversing shaping.

FRONT
Work as given for back from ★ to ★.
Continue in stripes until front measures 14 cm from beg, ending with a P row.
Shape neck
Next row: K17, turn and leave remaining sts on a spare needle.
Work straight on these sts until front measures same as back to shoulders, ending P row.
Cast off.
Return to sts on spare needle.
With right side facing, slip first 32 sts onto a holder, rejoin yarn to next st and complete to match first side of neck.

SLEEVES
Join shoulder seams.
With right side facing and using 2¾ mm needles and A, pick up and K67 sts between armhole markers.
P 1 row.

Beg with B, work in 2 row st st stripes for 8 rows, ending with a P row.
Change to 2¼ mm needles.
Beg rib row 2 and using A, work 5 rows rib.
Cast off knitwise.

NECK
With right side facing, set of four double pointed needles or circular needle and A, join yarn at back neck opening and K across 16 sts from holder, pick up and K25 sts up left back neck and down left front neck, K across 32 sts from holder, pick up and K26 sts up right side of front neck and down right back neck, then K across 16 sts from holder: 115 sts.
Working backwards and forwards in rows, work 5 rows in rib, dec 1 st either side of corner sts on next and every following alternate row.
Cast off purlwise.

TO MAKE UP
Join side and sleeve seams. Using 2·00 mm crochet hook and A, work 2 rows dc down left back opening and 4 rows down right back opening, making one 5 ch loop for buttonhole at top on right back. Sew on button. Slipstitch lower edges of opening neatly into place. Press following instructions on the ball band.

INSTRUCTIONS FOR TEDDY'S SHORTS

RIGHT LEG
Using 2¼ mm needles and A, cast on 75 sts.
Beg K row, work 6 rows in st st, change to 2¾ mm needles and work a further 6 rows.
Make hem as given for child's shorts.
Shape leg
Working in 2 row st st stripes, inc 1 st each end of 3rd and every following alternate row until there are 81 sts.
Work 1 row.
Shape back
Dec, 1 st at end of next and every following alternate row until 67 sts remain.
Work straight until leg measures 13 cm from beg, ending with a P row.
Break off yarn and leave sts on a spare needle.

LEFT LEG
Work as given for right leg, reversing all shaping, but do not break off yarn.

WAISTBAND
Next row: Using 2¼ mm needles and A, K across the first 66 sts of left leg, then working across sts of right leg, K tog the last st of left leg with first st of right leg, K across remaining 66 sts: 133 sts.
Beg P row, work a further 20 rows st st.
Cast off.
Complete as given for child's shorts.

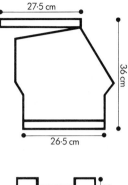

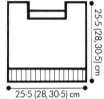

SUN HAT

A tiny mobcap knitted in one from brim to crown.

MEASUREMENTS
Actual measurement round hat 35·5(40·5,46,51) cm
[14(16,18,20) in]
Depth 10(12,12·5,14) cm

MATERIALS
1(1,2,2) × 50 g balls Phildar Perle No 5 or Fil
d'Ecosse
Shirring elastic
A pair each of 2 mm (No 14) and 2¾ mm (No 12)
knitting needles

TENSION
32 sts and 44 rows to 10 cm measured over st st
worked on 2¾ mm needles

INSTRUCTIONS

BRIM
Using 2¾ mm needles cast on 225(257,289,321) sts.
Row 1: K to end.
Row 2: K1, * yrn, K2 tog, rep from * to end.
Rows 3 and 4: K to end.
These 4 rows form patt. Rep them 4 times more.
Next row: * K2 tog, rep from * to last st, K1:
113(129,145, 161) sts. Now K 1 row.

CROWN
Change to 2 mm needles.
Using shirring elastic together with yarn, proceed as
follows:
Row 1: K1, * P1, K1, rep from * to end.
Row 2: K2, * P1, K1, rep from * to last st, K1.
Break off elastic.
Using yarn only, rep the last 2 rows three times more.
Change to 2¾ mm needles. Continue as follows:
* **Rows 1 to 3:** K to end.
Row 4: K1, * yrn, K2 tog, rep from * to end.
Rows 5 and 6: K to end. *
Beg with a K row, continue in st st until work
measures 10(12,12·5,14) cm from brim (including
ribbing).
Rep the 6 rows from * to * once more. Now K 2 rows.
Shape crown
Row 1: * K2 tog, rep from * to last st, K1: 57(65, 73,
81) sts.
Row 2 and every alternate row: K to end.
Row 3: As row 1: 29(33,37,41) sts.
Row 5: As row 1: 15(17,19,21) sts.
Row 7: As row 1: 8(9,10,11) sts, break off yarn
leaving a long length.
Thread yarn through sts, draw up tightly and fasten
off securely. Join side seam.

PEEKABOO

A holey beach top with tiny cap sleeves, a square neck
and shoulder fastening.

MEASUREMENTS
To fit chest 46 cm [18 in]
Actual measurement 46 cm
Length to shoulders 28 cm

MATERIALS
2 × 50 g balls Phildar Perle No 5 or Fil d'Ecosse
A pair of 2¾ mm (No 12) knitting needles
2 buttons

TENSION
24 sts to 10 cm measured over pattern

INSTRUCTIONS

BACK
★ Using 2¾ mm needles cast on 54 sts.
K 6 rows.
Work in patt as follows:
Row 1: (Right side) K to last st, sl last st.
Row 2: K1, * K2 tog, yrn, rep from * to last st, K1.
Rows 3 to 5: K to last st, sl last st.
Row 6: K1, * yrn, skpo, rep from * to last st, sl last st.
Rows 7 and 8: K to last st, sl last st.
These 8 rows form the patt.
Continue in patt until back measures 18 cm from
beg, ending with a wrong-side row.
Shape armholes
Next row: Cast on 4 sts, K these 4 sts then K to end of
row.
Next row: Cast on 4 sts, K these 4 sts, then K1, patt to
last 5 sts, K to end: 62 sts. ★
Keeping the 5 sts at each end worked in g st,
continue in patt until back measures 24 cm from beg,
ending with row 4 or 8 of patt.
★★ **Neck border**
Row 1: K to end.
Row 2: K5, patt across 10 sts, K32, patt across 10 sts,
K5.
Rows 3 to 5: K to end.
Divide for neck
Next row: K5, patt across 10 sts, K5, cast off 22 sts,
then K4, patt across 10 sts, K5.
Working on first set of sts, continue as follows:
K 3 rows.
Next row: K5, patt across 10 sts, K5. ★★
K 6 rows.
Cast off.
With right side facing, join yarn to remaining sts and
complete to match first side of neck, ending with K 7
rows instead of 6.
Cast off.

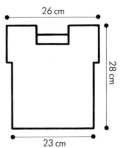

26 cm

28 cm

23 cm

When 'summer suns are glowing' this cotton sun hat will shade a little face, while the holey top will keep baby cool. Knitted in white, both look fresh and summery, but they would look just as cute in pale pastels.

FRONT

Work as given for back from ★ to ★.

Keeping the 5 sts at each end worked in g st, continue in patt until back measures 21·5 cm from beg, ending with a wrong-side row.

Now work neck border and shaping as given for back from ★★ to ★★.

Continue in patt, keeping g st borders correct until front measures same as back to beg of top border, ending with a wrong-side row.

K 8 rows.

Next row: (Buttonhole row) K5, yrn, K2 tog, K to last 7 sts, K2 tog, yrn, K5.

K 2 rows.

Cast off.

With right side facing, join yarn to remaining sts and complete to match first side ending with K 6 rows instead of 8.

Cast off.

TO MAKE UP

Join right shoulder seam. Join side and underarm seams

Sew on buttons to correspond with buttonholes.

BARNACLE BILL

A traditional Guernsey design – in miniature!

MEASUREMENTS

To fit chest 51(56) cm [20(22) in]
Actual measurements 61(66) cm
Length to shoulders 31(33·5) cm
Sleeve seam 23(25·5) cm

MATERIALS

250(300) g of Guernsey 5 ply
A pair of 2¼ mm (No 13) knitting needles
A set of four 2¼ mm (No 13) double pointed needles
or one circular 2¼ mm (No 13) needle

TENSION

32 sts and 44 rows to 10 cm measured over st st

SPECIAL TECHNIQUE

Guernsey grafting Hold the wrong sides of work together, with the points of the needles holding the stitches both facing the same way. Using a spare needle slip 1 st from each needle in turn onto the third needle until all stitches needed for grafting are on one needle, then cast off as follows:
[K2 tog] twice, pass the first st on right-hand needle over the second to cast it off, K the next 2 sts tog, then pass the first st on right-hand needle over the second again to cast it off, continue in this way until all the stitches are cast off.

INSTRUCTIONS

BACK

Using 2¼ mm needles cast on 90(102) sts.
Work 16 rows g st.
Proceed in rib as follows:
Rib row 1: K1, P1, K2, * P2, K2, rep from * to last 2 sts, P1, K1.
Rib row 2: * K2, P2, rep from * to last 2 sts, K2.
Rep these 2 rows twice more, then rib row 1 again.
Next row: (Right side) K15(21), * inc in next st, K9(14), rep from * to last 15(21)sts, inc in next st, K to end: 97(107) sts.
Next row: K1, P to last st, K1.
Always working K1 at each end of every P row, continue in st st until work measures 18(20·5) cm from beg, ending P row.
Place a marker at each end of last row to denote beg of armhole.
Now continue as follows:
Row 1: K6, P6, K to last 12 sts, P6, K6.
Row 2: K1, P to last st, K1.
Rep these 2 rows until work measures 30·5(33) cm from beg, ending row 2.
Cut off yarn and leave sts on a spare needle.

FRONT

Work as given for back.

NECK GUSSETS

Holding wrong sides of back and front together, slip the first 22(27) sts from each needle onto spare needles for first shoulder seam, and join together using the Guernsey grafting technique, do not fasten off but leave the final st on a spare needle for the neck gusset.
Slip 53 neck sts at centre of each piece onto spare needles, with points facing the grafted shoulder seam.
Using the needle with 1 st from shoulder grafting, K1 from the front needle holding 53 sts: 2 sts on right-hand needle, turn.
Next row: Sl the first st, P1, then P1 from second set of 53 sts: 3 sts on right-hand needle, turn.
Next row: Sl 1, then K2, K1 from first set of sts: 4 sts, turn.
Continue in this way, working across 1 more st each time until there are 11 sts on the needle.
Break yarn and leave these sts on a holder.
Graft the 2nd set of 22(27) shoulder sts and work neck gusset in same way as first.

NECKBAND

Using the set of four needles or circular needle, work 7 rounds in K2, P2 rib over all 108 sts on holders at neck.
Cast off purlwise.

SLEEVES

Using 2¼mm needles cast on 54 sts.
Rib row 1: * K2, P2, rep from * to last 2 sts, K2.
Rib row 2: K1, P1, K2, * P2, K2, rep from * to last 2 sts, P1, K1.
Rep these 2 rows for 5(6·5) cm, ending rib row 2.
Work in st st, inc 1 st each end of next and every following 4th row until there are 82 sts.
Work straight until sleeve measures 21·5(24) cm from beg, ending P row.
Work 7 rows in rib as given for cuff.
Cast off knitwise.

UNDERARM GUSSETS

Using 2¼ mm needles cast on 1 st.
Working in st st, inc 1 st at beg of every row until there are 13 sts, then dec 1 st at beg of every row until 1 st remains.
Fasten off.

TO MAKE UP

Sew in sleeves between markers, then sew in underarm gussets.
Leaving lower edges open below ribbing, join side and sleeve seams.
Press lightly following instructions on ball band.

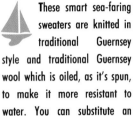 These smart sea-faring sweaters are knitted in traditional Guernsey style and traditional Guernsey wool which is oiled, as it's spun, to make it more resistant to water. You can substitute an ordinary yarn of the same weight if you prefer.

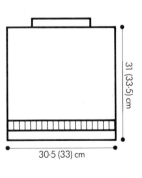

31 (33·5) cm

30·5 (33) cm

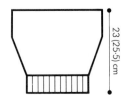

23 (25·5) cm

BEACH BABY

Easy-fitting beach pants with bib.

MEASUREMENTS
To fit waist 46(51) cm [18(20) in]
Waist to crutch 20·5(23) cm

MATERIALS
2 × 50 g balls Phildar Skate
A pair each of 2¾ mm (No 12) and 3¼ mm (No 10)
knitting needles
2 buttons
Waist length of elastic

TENSION
22 sts and 32 rows to 10 cm measured over st st
worked on 3¼ mm needles

INSTRUCTIONS

FRONT
Starting at bib.
Using 3¼ mm needles cast on 25(29) sts.
Moss st row: K1, * P1, K1, rep from * to end.
Repeating this row forms the moss st patt.
Moss st 1 more row.
Next row: (Buttonhole row) K1, Pl, yrn, K2 tog, moss
st to last 4 sts, K2 tog, yrn, P1, K1.
Moss st 3 more rows.
Next row: Moss st 5, K15(19), moss st 5.
Next row: Moss st 5, P15(19), moss st 5.
Rep the last 2 rows until bib measures 10(11·5)cm
from beg, ending with a wrong-side row.
Change to 2¾ mm needles.
Next row: Cast on 14 sts, [K1, P1] to last st, K1.
Next row: Cast on 14 sts, [K1, P1] to last st, K1:
53(57)sts.
★★ Now work rib casing for elastic as follows:
Row 1: * K1, yf, sl 1 pw, yb, rep from * to last st, K1.
Row 2: K1, * K1, yf, sl 1 pw, yb, rep from * to last
2 sts, K2.
Rep these 2 rows 3 times more.
Change to 3¼ mm needles.
Beg K row, work in st st until front measures
12.5(15) cm from beg of rib casing, ending with a K
row.
Divide for legs
Row 1: (Wrong side) K1, P16(17), turn and leave
remaining sts on a spare needle.
Row 2: K3, K2 tog, K to end.
Row 3: K1, P10(11), P2 tog, K3.
Row 4: As row 2.
Continue dec 1 st inside g st border in this way until
1 st remains.
Fasten off.
Return to sts on spare needle.

With wrong side facing, join yarn to first st, P to last
st, K1.
Continue as follows:
Row 1: K12(13), K2 tog, K3, turn and leave
remaining sts on a spare needle.
Row 2: K3, P2 tog, P to last st, K1.
Row 3: K10(11), K2 tog, K3.
Row 4: As row 2.
Continue dec 1 st inside g st border in this way until
1 st remains. Fasten off.
Return to sts on spare needle.
With right side facing, join yarn to first st and
continue as follows:
Row 1: K to end.
Row 2: K3, P to last 3 sts, K3.
Rep these 2 rows 4 times more.
Still working 3 sts in g st at each end of the row, inc 1
st at each end of every row until there are 53(57)sts,
ending with a wrong-side row.
Place a marker at each end of last row to denote
end of front leg shaping.
Now continue with back as follows:
Beg with a K row, work in st st until back measures
same as front from markers to beg of rib casing,
ending P row.
Change to 2¾ mm needles.
Now work rib casing for elastic as follows:
Row 1: * K1, yf, sl 1 pw, yb, rep from * to last st, K1.
Row 2: K1, * K1, yf, sl 1 pw, yb, rep from * to last 2
sts, K2.
Rep these 2 rows 3 times more, then row 1 again.
Next row: K1, * P1, K1, rep from * to end. ★★
Divide for straps
With right side facing, cast off 12(14), then [P1, K1] 3
times, cast off 15, then [P1, K1] 3 times, cast off
remaining 12(14) sts.
Using 3¼ mm needles, join yarn to first set of 7 sts
for strap and work in moss st until strap measures
25·5 cm from beg.
Shape end
Row 1: K2 tog, moss st to last 2 sts, K2 tog.
Row 2: Moss st to end.
Row 3: As row 1.
Cast off remaining 3 sts.
Work 2nd strap to match first.

TO MAKE UP
Join side seams, sew on buttons. Thread elastic (if
required) through each section of casing and secure
at each end.

Cheerful seaside colours will flatter any bright-eyed beach baby. If the bib and straps on these beach pants seem over stretchy, they can be reinforced with a fabric or ribbon lining for extra strength.

25·5 cm

17·5 (20) cm

12·5 (15) cm

10 (11·5) cm

24 (26) cm

BOTTOMS UP!

A version of the beach pants but without the bib.

MEASUREMENTS
To fit waist 46(51) cm [18(20) in]
Waist to crutch 20·5(23) cm

MATERIALS
2 × 50 g balls Phildar Skate
A pair each of 2¾ mm (No 12) and 3¼ mm (No 10)
knitting needles; waist length of elastic

TENSION
22 sts and 32 rows to 10 cm measured over st st
worked on 3¼ mm needles

INSTRUCTIONS

FRONT
Using 2¾ mm needles cast on 53(57) sts.
Rib row 1: K1, ✶ P1, K1, rep from ✶ to end.
Rib row 2: P1, ✶ K1, P1 rep from ✶ to end.
Now work as given for Beach Baby bibbed pants
from ✶✶ to ✶✶.
Cast off.

TO MAKE UP
Join side seams.
Thread elastic (if required) through each section of
casing and secure at each end.
Press according to instructions on the ball band.

"Dance to your daddy,
My little babby,
Dance to your daddy,
My little lamb.

You shall have a fishy,
In a little dishy,
You shall have a fishy,
When the boat comes in."

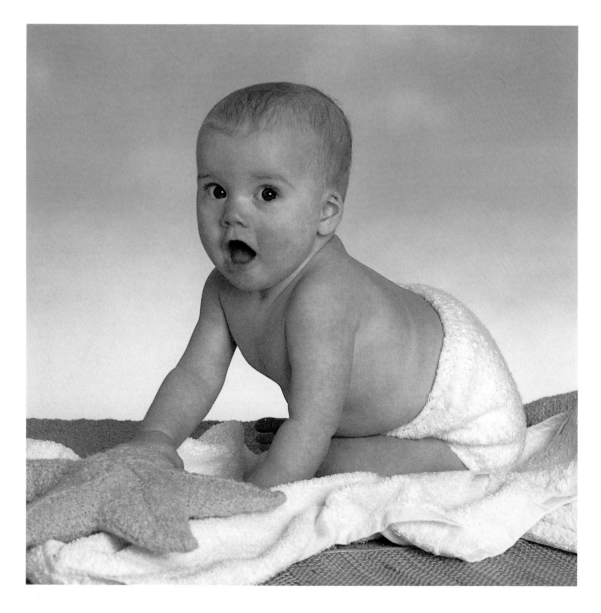

STELLA STARFISH

The starfish's five points are knitted separately, then picked up on to double-pointed needles and worked in rounds until completed.

MEASUREMENTS
Actual measurements approximately 25·5(41) cm [10(16) in] diameter

MATERIALS
1(2) × 50 g balls Phildar Skate
A pair of 3¼ mm (No 10) and a set of four double-pointed 3¼ mm (No 10) knitting needles for the small starfish
A pair of 4½ mm (No 7) and a set of four double-pointed 4½ mm (No 7) knitting needles for the large starfish
Foam chips for filling

TENSION
22 sts and 32 rows to 10 cm measured over st st worked on 3¼ mm needles using 1 strand of yarn

NOTE
The small starfish is knitted using 1 strand of yarn and the 3¼ mm needles throughout and the larger starfish is knitted to the same pattern using 2 strands of yarn together and the 4½ mm needles throughout.

INSTRUCTIONS

UNDERSIDE
✶ Using the 3¼ mm needles and 1 strand of yarn for the small star or the 4½ mm needles and 2 strands of yarn for the large star, cast on 3 sts.
Working in rev st st throughout, inc 1 st at each end of the 5th and every following 4th row until there are 13 sts.
Work 9 rows straight. [Work should measure 10(15) cm] Break off yarn and leave sts on a spare needle.
Make 4 more pieces in the same way but do not break off yarn on last piece.
Next row: P across 13 sts on needle, then P across 13 sts of each of the other 4 pieces: 65 sts.
Next row: K to end. ✶
Arrange sts onto three of the set of four double-pointed needles and work in rounds as follows:
Round 1: P4, P2 tog, ✶ P11, P2 tog, rep from ✶ to last 7 sts, P7: 60 sts.
Round 2 and every alternate round: P to end.
Round 3: P3, P2 tog, ✶ P10, P2 tog, rep from ✶ to last 7 sts, P7: 55 sts.
Continue dec in this way, working 1 st less between each dec, until 20 sts remain, and ending with a plain P round.

Next round: ✶ P2 tog, rep from ✶ to end: 10 sts. Break off yarn, thread through sts and draw up tightly, then fasten off securely.

TOPSIDE
Keeping centre st of each of the five points in st st (showing as a knit st on the right side) throughout, work as given for underside from ✶ to ✶.
Arrange sts onto 3 of the set of four double-pointed needles and work in rounds as follows:
Round 1: P6, K1, P2 tog, ✶ P10, K1, P2 tog, rep from ✶ to last 4 sts, P4.
Round 2 and every alternate round: P all the purl sts and K all the knit sts to the end.
Round 3: P6, K1, P2 tog, ✶ P9, K1, P2 tog, rep from ✶ to last 3 sts, P3.
Continuing to dec after each K st in this way, complete as given for underside.

TO MAKE UP
Placing right sides together, join outer edges, leaving a small section open for filling. Turn to right side, fill firmly with foam chips and close opening securely.

Filled with foam chips – or chopped up (old!) tights or stockings – this unusual knitted starfish is washable, chewable and virtually indestructible. What more could you ask for in a beach toy?

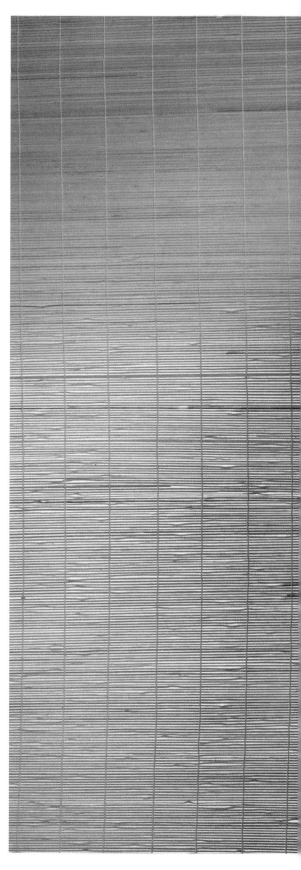

BEACH BELLE

The sundress (with or without anchors) is made from two identical pieces — back and front — which are joined at the sides. In both of these pieces the skirt and top are continuous. You simply reduce the number of stitches by half at the waist band!

MEASUREMENTS
To fit chest 46(51,56) cm [18(20,22) in]
Actual measurements 51(56,61) cm
Length to shoulders 40·5(43,46) cm

MATERIALS
3(4,4) × 50 g balls Phildar Perle No 5 or Fil d'Ecosse in main colour A
1 ball same in contrast colour B (if motifs required)
A pair each of 2¼ mm (No 13) and 2¾ mm (No 12) knitting needles
Two short double-pointed 2¼ mm (No 13) knitting needles for tubular knitting

TENSION
32 sts and 44 rows to 10 cm measured over st st worked on 2¾ mm needles

SPECIAL TECHNIQUE
Tubular Knitting Using double pointed needles and working over 5 sts, K 1 row.
Do not turn work but slip the 5 sts to the other end of the needle, bring the yarn across the back of the work and pulling yarn tightly K the row again from right to left.
Continue in this way, always keeping the right side of the fabric facing and always working from right to left across the work thus creating a tubular piece of knitting.

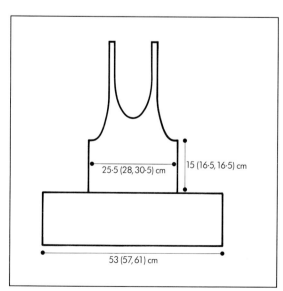

25·5 (28, 30·5) cm
15 (16·5, 16·5) cm
53 (57, 61) cm

With or without the anchor motifs, these simple little sundresses are cool and comfy. They begin with a picot edge, the skirts are in stocking stitch, the tops in reversed stocking stitch and the ties in tubular knitting – what could be simpler?

□ = A   ● = B

12 st patt rep

INSTRUCTIONS

BACK AND FRONT (alike)

Using 2¼ mm needles and A, cast on
171(183,195) sts.
Beg K row, work 8 rows st st.
Next row: K1, * yrn, K2 tog, rep from * to end.
Change to 2¾ mm needles.
Beg P row, work 9 rows st st.
With wrong sides together, fold work along eyelet
hole row and make hem as follows:
Next row: K1, pick up first loop from cast-on edge
and K tog with next st on left-hand needle, * pick up
next loop from cast-on edge and K tog with the next
st on left-hand needle, rep from * to end.
Work 3 rows st st.
Now working from chart, place motifs (if required)
as follows:
Row 1: K6A, * 3B, 9A rep from * to last 9 sts, 3B, 6A.
Row 2: P5A, * 1B, 1A, 1B, 1A, 1B, 7A, rep from * to
last 10 sts, 1B, 1A, 1B, 1A, 1B, 5A.
Continue in this way working from chart until row 12
has been completed.
Break off B.
Using A only, continue in st st until skirt measures
14(15,18)cm (or length desired) from beg, ending
with a wrong-side row.
Dec row: K1, * K2 tog, rep from * to end:
86(92,98)sts.
Next row: K to end.
Beg P row, work in rev st st until bodice measures
15(16·5,16·5)cm from dec row, ending K row.
★ Shape armholes
Cast off 4 sts at beg of next 2 rows: 78(84,90) sts.
Dec 1 st each end of every row to 60(66,72) sts, then
at each end of every following alternate row until
52(58,64) sts remain, ending K row.
Work 2 rows straight.
Shape neck
Next row: (Right side) P21(24,26), cast off next
10(10,12) sts, P to end.
Working on first set of sts only, dec 1 st at neck edge
on next and every following alternate row until 5 sts
remain.
Work 1 row, then changing to double pointed
needles, work 18(20,20) cm of tubular knitting.
Break off yarn and thread through sts, draw up tight
and fasten off securely.
Return to remaining sts.
With wrong side facing, join yarn to first st and
complete to match first side of neck.

TO MAKE UP

Join side seams.
Press skirt carefully according to instructions on ball
band.
Allowing neck and armhole edges to roll, tie straps
into a bow to fit. ★

SUN TOP

This cheeky little sun top is created by losing the skirt
from the sundress, but otherwise it's knitted in exactly
the same way.

MEASUREMENTS

To fit chest 46(51,56) cm [18(20,22) in]
Actual measurements 51(56,61) cm
Length to shoulders 25·5(28,30·5) cm

MATERIALS

2 × 50 g balls Phildar Perle No 5 or Fil d'Ecosse
A pair each of 2¼ mm (No 13) and 2¾ mm (No 12)
knitting needles
Two short double-pointed 2¼ mm (No 13) knitting
needles for tubular knitting

TENSION

32 sts and 44 rows to 10 cm measured over st st
worked on 2¾ mm needles

SPECIAL TECHNIQUE

Tubular Knitting Using double pointed needles and
working over 5 sts, K 1 row.
Do not turn work but slip the 5 sts to the other end of
the needle, bring the yarn across the back of the
work and pulling yarn tightly K the row again
from right to left.
Continue in this way, always keeping the right side
of the fabric facing and always working from right to
left across the working thus creating a tubular piece
of knitting.

INSTRUCTIONS

BACK AND FRONT (alike)

Using 2¼ mm needles cast on 85(91,97)sts.
Rib row 1: K1, * P1, K1, rep from * to end.
Rib row 2: K2, * P1, K1, rep from * to last st, K1.
Rep these 2 rows for 2·5 cm, inc 1 st at end of last
row: 86(92,98) sts.
Change to 2¾ mm needles.
Beg P row, work in rev st st until top measures
11·5(14,16·5) cm from beg, ending with a K row.
Now complete as given for the Beach Belle sundress
from ★ to ★.

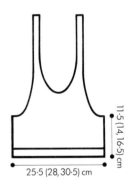

11·5 (14, 16·5) cm

25·5 (28, 30·5) cm

*T*EDDY BEARS

This chapter is devoted to bears. There are jumpers and dungarees with teddy bear motifs, a family of three bears to knit and garments inspired by teddy colours and textures. As every one knows, children adore teddy bears; big or small, fat or thin, furry or fuzzy, they are the most popular of all nursery toys. So, it's hardly surprising that in this section the bears take over!

FUZZY WUZZY

A long-sleeved jumper with a shirt-collar fastening and teddy bear motifs around the body.

MEASUREMENTS
To fit chest 46(51,56) cm [18(20,22) in]
Actual measurements 53(58,63) cm
Length to shoulders 28·5(30,33) cm
Sleeve seam 18(20·5,23) cm

MATERIALS
2(3,3) × 20g balls Woolgatherers Radiangor in main colour A
1 ball same in contrast colour B
A pair each of 2 mm (No 14) and 2¾ mm (No 12) knitting needles
3 buttons

TENSION
34 sts and 47 rows to 10 cm measured over st st worked on 2¾ mm needles

INSTRUCTIONS

BACK
★ Using 2 mm needles and B, cast on 85(93,101) sts.
Rib row 1: K2, ★ P1, K1, rep from ★ to last st, K1.
Rib row 2: K1, ★ P1, K1, rep from ★ to end.
Rep these 2 rows for 3(3,4) cm, ending rib row 2.
Change to 2¾ mm needles.

Knitted in teddy bear shades of an angora or angora-mix yarn, this furry jumper will enable any child to join the pack! If you are going to knit this for a baby, a slightly brushed woollen yarn might be more advisable as angora yarns can be rather fluffy.

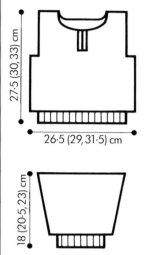

27·5 (30, 33) cm

26·5 (29, 31·5) cm

18 (20·5, 23) cm

Break off B and join on A.

Inc row: K10(12, 13), ✷ inc in next st, K12(13,14), rep from ✷ to last 10(11,13) sts, inc in next st, K to end: 91(99,107) sts. P1 row. ★

Beg with a K row, work in st st until back measures 16·5(18,19) cm from beg, ending with a P row.

Shape armholes

Cast off 8 sts at beg of next 2 rows: 75(83,91) sts.
Work straight until back measures 26·5(29,32) cm from beg, ending with a P row.

Shape neck

Next row: K19(23,25), K2 tog, K2, turn and leave remaining sts on a spare needle.

Next row: P2, P2 tog, P to end.

Continue to dec 1 st in this way at neck edge until 17(21,23) sts remain, changing to B on the last row. Using B, cast off. Return to remaining sts.
With right side facing, slip first 29(29,33) sts onto a holder, join yarn to remaining sts and complete to match first side of neck, reversing all shaping.

FRONT

Work as given for back from ★ to ★ .
Beg with a K row, work 4 rows st st.
Using separate small balls of yarn for each Teddy motif, place motifs from chart as follows:

Row 1: K13(17,21)A, [5B, 7A] 5 times, 5B, 13(17,21)A.

Row 2: P12(16,20)A, [7B, 5A] 5 times, 7B, 12(16,20)A.

Continue in patt from chart until row 26 has been completed.
Working in A only, continue in st st until front measures same as back to armhole shaping, ending with a P row.

Shape armholes

Cast off 8 sts at beg of next 2 rows: 75(83,91) sts.
K1 row.

Divide for front opening

Next row: P34(38,42), turn and leave remaining sts on a spare needle.

Next row: Join on B and cast on 7 sts, [K1, P1] 3 times, K1, for button border, change back to A and K to end: 41(45,49) sts.

Twisting yarns together at back of work when changing colour, continue in st st with A and moss st with B until front measures 20 rows less than back to shoulders, ending at neck edge.

Shape neck

Next row: Moss st 7B, K5(5,7)A then slip these 12(12,14) sts onto a safety-pin, work across 2 sts, work 2 tog, work to end.

Continue dec 1 st at neck edge, within the 2 st border, on every row until 17(21,23) sts remain.
Work straight until front measures same as back to shoulders, working last row in B.
Using B, cast off.
Mark the positions for 2 buttons on this border, the first one 7 rows from beg of button border, then allowing for the 3rd one to be on the neckband, place the other one evenly between.
Return to remaining sts.
With wrong side facing, join B to first st, P7B, join on A and P to end: 41(45,49) sts.

Next row: K34(38,42)A, moss st 7B.

Now complete to match first side reversing all shaping and working buttonholes to correspond with markers as follows:

Buttonhole row: (Wrong side) With B, K1, P1, K1, yrn, skpo, P1, K1, then with A K to end.

SLEEVES

Using 2 mm needles and B, cast on 45(49,53) sts.
Work 3(3,4) cm in rib as given for back.

Inc row: K1(3,4), ✷ inc in next st, K5, rep from ✷ to last 2(4,7) sts, inc in next st, K to end: 53(57,61) sts.

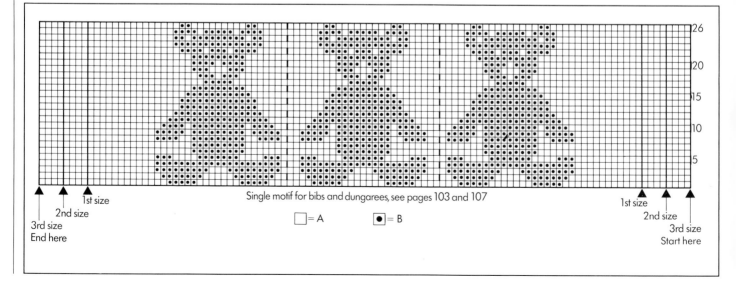

1st size
2nd size
3rd size
End here

Single motif for bibs and dungarees, see pages 103 and 107

□ = A   ● = B

1st size
2nd size
3rd size
Start here

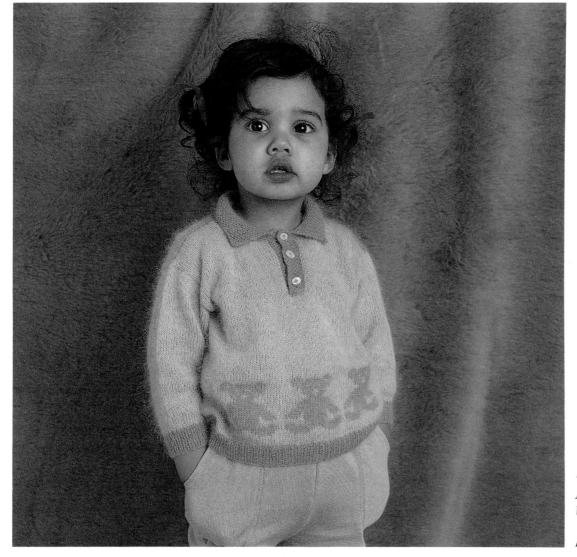

*'Fuzzy Wuzzy was a bear,
A bear was Fuzzy Wuzzy.
When Fuzzy Wuzzy lost his
    fur,
He wasn't fuzzy wuz he?'*

Change to 2¾ mm needles.
Break off B.
Join on A.
Beg P row and working in st st, inc 1 st each end of
5th and every following 4th row until there are
75(83,91) sts.
Work straight until sleeve measures 18(20·5,23) cm
from beg.
Cast off.

NECKBAND AND COLLAR
(worked in one piece)
Join shoulder seams.
With right side facing and using 2 mm needles and
B, moss st across 12(12,14) sts from safety-pin at
right front, pick up and K18 sts up right side of front
neck and 5 sts down right side of back neck, K
across 29(29,33) sts from back neck holder, pick up
and K5 sts up left side of back neck and 18 sts down

left side of front neck, then moss st across
12(12,14) sts from safety-pin at left front:
99(99,107) sts.
Next row: Moss st to end.
Next row: Moss st to last 4 sts, yrn, skpo, P1, K1.
Work 4 moss st.
Next row: Cast off 4 sts knitwise, moss st to end.
Next row: Cast off 4 sts purlwise, moss st to end:
91(91,99) sts.
Work 5 cm in moss st, ending with a right-side row.
Cast off knitwise.

TO MAKE UP
Fold sleeves in half lengthwise, then placing folds to
shoulder seams, sew in sleeves.
Join side and sleeve seams.
Sew lower edge of button band neatly into place.
Sew on buttons to correspond with buttonholes.
Press lightly following instructions on ball band.

PLAYTIME

A high-waisted dress with a distinctive wide collar.

MEASUREMENTS
To fit chest 50(56,61) cm [20(22,24) in]
Length to shoulders 41(44,47) cm
Sleeve seam 25(26,27) cm

MATERIALS
5 × 50 g balls Pingouin Pingofine in main colour A
2 × 50 g balls Pingouin Skate in contrast colour B
2 × 50 g balls Pingouin Comfortable Fin in contrast colour C
A pair each of 2 mm (No 14) and 2¼ mm (No 13) knitting needles
One 2¼ mm (No 13) circular needle
2·50 mm (No 12) crochet hook

TENSION
59 sts and 46 rows to 10 cm measured over rib worked on 2¼ mm needles with Pingofine
32 sts and 44 rows to 10 cm measured over st st worked on 2¼ mm needles with Skate

INSTRUCTIONS

SKIRT
Using 2¼ mm circular needle and A, cast on 404(440,476) sts.
Working backwards and forwards in rows, work in K1, P1 rib for 12 rows.
Continuing in rib, work 2 rows C, 22 rows A, 2 rows B and 70(82,94) rows A.
Next row: (Dec row) ✻ K3 tog, rep from ✻ to last 2 sts, K2 tog: 135(147,159) sts.
Cast off.

BODICE AND SLEEVES
Using 2¼ mm needles and A, cast on 88 sts.
Work 24 rows in K2, P2 rib.
Inc row: (Right side) [K1, P1] into each st to end: 176 sts.
Now continuing in K1, P1 rib and inc 1 st each end of next and every following 3rd row until there are 212 sts, work 3 rows A, 2 rows B, 22 rows A, 2 rows C and 23 rows A.
Using A only, work 38(44,50) rows in rib.
Place a marker at each end of last row to denote beg of bodice.
Break off A and join on B.
Row 1: (Wrong side) P4, ✻ P1, [P2 tog] 8 times, rep from ✻ to last st, P4: 116 sts.
Beg with a K row, work 10 rows st st.
Divide for neck
Next row: K55, K2 tog, K1, turn and leave remaining 58 sts on a spare needle.

Continue on these 57 sts for back bodice.
Next row: P.
Next row: K to last 3 sts, K2 tog, K1.
Rep the last 2 rows twice more: 54 sts.
Work 74(86,96) rows st st.
Next row: K to last 2 sts, inc in next st, K1.
Next row: P.
Next row: K to last 2 sts, inc in next st, K1.
Rep the last 2 rows twice more: 58 sts.
Break off yarn and leave sts on a holder.
Return to sts on spare needle.
With right side facing, join on B, K1, K2 tog, K to end: 57 sts.
Next row: P.
Next row: K1, K2 tog, K to end of row.
Rep last 2 rows 4 times more: 52 sts.
Work 66(78,88) rows st st.
Next row: K1, inc in next st, K to end.
Next row: P.
Next row: K1, inc in next st, K to end.
Rep last 2 rows 4 times more: 58 sts.
Next row: P58 sts, then P across 58 sts from holder 116 sts.
Work 10 rows st st. Break off B and join on A.
Next row: (Inc row) K4, ✻ K1, [inc in next st] 8 times, rep from ✻ to last st, K4: 212 sts.
Place a marker at each end of last row to denote end of bodice.
Work 38(44,50) rows K1, P1 rib.
Continuing in rib and decreasing 1 st each end of next and every following 3rd row until 176 sts remain, work 23 rows A, 2 rows C, 22 rows A, 2 rows B and 3 rows A.
Continuing in A only, work cuff as follows:
Next row: ✻ [K2 tog] twice, [P2 tog] twice, rep from ✻ to end: 88 sts.
Now work 24 rows K2, P2 rib. Cast off in rib.

Bright colours make this into a stunning little play dress. It's loose-fitting and has long sleeves and an unusual wide collar. The pattern for Teddy's bib is on page 103.

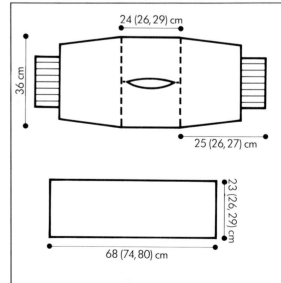

24 (26, 29) cm

36 cm

25 (26, 27) cm

23 (26, 29) cm

68 (74, 80) cm

COLLAR

With wrong side facing and using 2¼ mm circular needle, join C to front neck approximately 6 cm in from left shoulder then pick up and K15(20,25) sts across to left shoulder, 50(67,72) sts across back neck, then 35(41,47) sts across front neck: 100(122,144) sts.

Inc row: Using A, P into back and front of next 2 sts, then using C, P into back and front of each st to end: 196(240,284) sts.

Always twisting A and C together when changing colour, continue in rib as follows:

Rib row 1: With C, K4, ☆ P2, K2, rep from ☆ to last 6 sts, P2, then with A K4.

Rib row 2: With A, P4, then with C, K2, ☆ P2, K2, rep from ☆ to last 6 sts, P2, K4.

Rep these 2 rows 16(17,18) times more.
Cast off in rib.

TO MAKE UP

Join centre back skirt seam. Join sleeve seams to markers. Sew skirt to Bodice. Sew button to left front collar edge.

INSTRUCTIONS FOR BAG

Using 2¼ mm needles cast on 5 sts in A, 20 sts in B and 5 sts in A: 30 sts.

Row 1: With A [K1, P1] twice, K1, with B K20, with A [K1, P1] twice, K1.

Row 2: With A [P1, K1] twice, P1, with B P20, with A [P1, K1] twice, P1.

Rep these 2 rows 4 times more. (84 rows altogether.)

Next row: In A only, [K1, P1] twice, K22, [P1, K1] twice.

Next row: In A only, [P1, K1] twice, P22, [K1, P1] twice.

Now rep rows 1 and 2 five times more.

Next row: In C only, [K1, P1] twice, K22, [P1, K1] twice.

Next row: In C only, [P1, K1] twice, P22, [K1, P1] twice.

Now rep rows 1 and 2 once.

Working in B only and st st, dec 1 st each end of next 7 rows: 16 sts.

Next row: P2 tog, P4, cast off 4 sts, P to last 2 sts, P2 tog.

Next row: K2 tog, K3, cast on 4 sts, K to last 2 sts, K2 tog.

Continue to dec 1 st each end of every row until 2 sts remain.
Cast off.

TO MAKE UP

Fold bag across width approximately 10 cm from cast-on edge and join side seams. Fold flap over at top and sew on button to correspond with buttonhole. Using A, crochet a chain to form strap to the length required. Stitch strap to top of bag.

THE THREE BEARS

The Three Bears of nursery fame: Daddy Bear, Mummy Bear and Baby Bear.

MEASUREMENTS

Height approximately 30(40,50) cm [12(16,20) in]

MATERIALS

1(2,3) × 50 g balls King Cole Superwash 4 ply
A pair of 2¾ mm (No 12) knitting needles for the small bear, 3¾ mm (No 9) for the medium bear and 5 mm (No 6) for the large bear
A small length of black yarn for embroidering features
Washable filling
Ribbon for bows if desired

TENSION

31 sts and 41 rows to 10 cm measured over st st worked on 2¾ mm needles using 1 strand
23 sts and 28 rows to 10 cm measured over st st worked on 3¾ mm needles using 2 strands
18 sts and 22 rows to 10 cm measured over st st worked on 5 mm needles using 3 strands

NOTE

The pattern for all three bears is the same, the size being altered by using 1 strand of yarn for the small bear 2 strands of yarn for the medium bear and 3 bear strands of yarn for the large bear.

INSTRUCTIONS FOR TEDDIES

BODY

Using 2¾(3¾,5) mm needles and 1(2,3) strands of yarn, cast on 32 sts.
Beg K row work 32 rows st st.

Shape shoulders
Dec 1 st each end of every row until 18 sts remain.
Work 1 row.

Shape face and nose
Row 1: Inc in first st, K7, M1, K2, M1, K7, inc into last st: 22 sts.
Row 2 and every alternate row: P.
Row 3: Inc in first st, K9, M1, K2, M1, K9, inc in last st: 26 sts.
Row 5: Inc in first st, K11, M1, K2, M1, K11, inc in last st: 30 sts.
Row 7: Inc in first st, K13, M1, K2, M1, K13, inc in last st: 34 sts.
Row 9: K16, M1, K2, M1, K16: 36 sts.
Row 11: K17, M1, K2, M1, K17: 38 sts.
Row 12: P.

Shape top of nose
Row 1: K17, K2 tog, K2 tog tbl, K17.
Row 2 and every alternate row: P.

Row 3: K16, K2 tog, K2 tog tbl, K16.
Row 5: K15, K2 tog, K2 tog tbl, K15.
Row 7: K14, K2 tog, K2 tog tbl, K14.
Row 9: K13, K2 tog, K2 tog tbl, K13.
Row 11: K12, K2 tog, K2 tog tbl, K12.
Row 12: P to end: 26 sts.
Shape top of head
Dec 1 st each end of next and every following alternate row until 18 sts remain.
Work 1 row.
Back of head
Inc 1 st each end of next and every following alternate row until there are 26 sts.
Work 15 rows straight, so ending with a P row.

Shape neck
Dec 1 st each end of next and every following alternate row until 18 sts remain.
Work 2 rows.
Shape shoulders
Inc 1 st each end of next 7 rows: 32 sts.
Back
Work 32 rows straight.
Divide for legs
Next row: Cast on 16 sts, K these 16 sts, then K16, turn and leave remaining sts on a spare needle.
Work 38 rows st st on these 32 sts.
Sole
K 4 rows.

No chapter on teddies would be complete without the Three Bears. Each of these is knitted from exactly the same pattern. Simply increase the strands of yarn; use one for the small bear, two for the medium-sized bear and three for the large bear.

Shape sole
Next row: [K2 tog] 16 times.
K 3 rows.
Next row: [K2 tog] 8 times: 8 sts.
Break off yarn leaving a long length, thread through sts, then draw up tightly and fasten off securely.
Return to remaining sts.
With right side facing, join on yarn and K16, turn and cast on 16 sts.
Now complete to match first leg.

ARMS
Using 2¾(3¾,5) mm needles and 1(2,3) strands of yarn, cast on 12 sts.
Beg with a K row and working in st st, inc 1 st each end of every row until there are 24 sts.
Work 32 rows straight.
Shape end of arms
K4 rows.
Next row: [K2 tog] 12 times.
K 3 rows.
Next row: [K2 tog] 6 times: 6 sts.
Break off yarn leaving a long length, thread through sts, then draw up tightly and fasten off securely.

EARS
Using 2¾(3¾,5) mm needles and 1(2,3) strands of yarn, cast on 6 sts.
Beg with a K row and working in st st, inc 1 st each end of every row until there are 14 sts.
Work 4 rows straight.
Dec 1 st each end of next and every alternate row until 8 sts remain, so ending with a K row.
K1 row to make a ridge on right side.
Continuing in st st, inc 1 st each end of every row until there are 14 sts.
Work 5 rows straight.
Dec 1 st each end of every row until 6 sts remain.
Cast off.

TO MAKE UP
Using length of black yarn, embroider eyes, nose and mouth following diagram above.
Join leg seams, then fill firmly. Join lower edge of front body to tops of legs, then join body and head seams, leaving a small opening. Fill body, head and neck firmly, then sew to body at shoulders. Fold ears in half and join side seams, then stitch into place.

Where else would you expect to find bears but in the woods? These particular bears (opposite) are rather shy and only peep out from behind the trees. This makes them great favourites with toddlers who love to spot them!

BEARS IN THE WOOD

A colourful jumper with a delightful tree and bear motif.

MEASUREMENTS
To fit chest 51(56) cm [20(22) in]
Actual measurements 64(69) cm
Length to shoulders 36(40) cm
Sleeve seam 23(26) cm

MATERIALS
3(3,4) × 50 g balls Patons Diploma 4 ply in main colour A
1(1,2) balls same in contrast colour B
1 ball each of same in contrast colours C, D and E
A pair each of 2¾ mm (No 12) and 3¼ mm (No 10) knitting needles
3 buttons

TENSION
28 sts and 36 rows to 10 cm measured over st st worked on 3¼ mm needles

INSTRUCTIONS

BACK
Using 2¾ mm needles and A, cast on 69(77) sts.
Rib row 1: K1, ✳ P1, K1, rep from ✳ to end.
Rib row 2: P1, ✳ K1, P1, rep from ✳ to end.
Rep these 2 rows for 5 cm, ending with rib row 1.
Inc row: Rib 6(5), ✳ M1, rib 3, M1, rib 3(4), rep from ✳ to last 3(2) sts, rib to end: 89(97) sts. Change to 3¼ mm needles. Beg K row, work 4 rows st st.
Using separate balls of yarn for each motif and twisting yarns together at back of work when changing colour to avoid making a hole, proceed to place first and 2nd motifs as follows:
Row 1: K3(5)A, working from chart [K10A, 5C, 10A], K33(37)A, working from chart [K10A, 5C, 10A], then K3(5)A.
Row 2: P3(5)A, working from chart [P10A, 5C, 10A], P33(37)A, working from chart [P10A, 5C, 10A], then P3(5)A.
Continue working motifs from chart as established until row 18 has been completed.
Now continuing to work motifs as set place 3rd motif in between first two as follows:
Next row: K3(5)A, patt across row 19 of chart, K4(6)A, working from row 1 of chart [K10A, 5C, 10A], K4(6)A, patt across row 19 of chart, then K3(5)A.
Continue in patt as now set until row 38 of first 2 motifs has been completed, then continue with 3rd motif only for a further 6 rows.
Now place 4th and 5th motifs at the same position in the row as first and second and continue in patt until row 38 of third motif has been completed, then

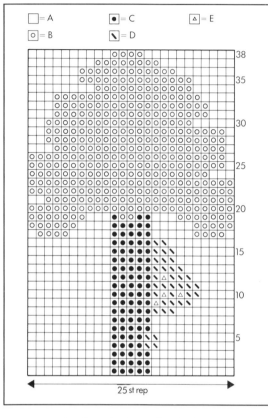

□ = A		⊙ = C		△ = E	
⊡ = B		◣ = D			

38
35
30
25
20
15
10
5

← 25 st rep →

continue with 4th and 5th motifs only for a further 6 rows. Continue in this way, placing the 6th motif above the 3rd, then the 7th and 8th above the 4th and 5th, working 6 rows in between, until row 18(32) of the 7th and 8th motifs has been worked.

Shape shoulders

Cast off 14(15) st at beg of next 4 rows.
Break off yarn and leave remaining 33(37) sts on a holder.

FRONT

Work as given for back until front measures 26 rows less than back to shoulders, so ending with a wrong-side row.

Shape neck

Next row: Patt across 36(38) sts, turn and leave remaining sts on a holder.
Dec 1 st at neck edge on the next 3 rows, then on every following alternate row until 28(30) sts remain.
Work straight until front measures same as back to shoulder, ending at armhole edge.

Shape shoulder

Cast off 14(15) sts at beg of next row.
Work 1 row, then cast off.
Return to remaining sts.
With right side facing, slip first 17(21) sts onto a holder, rejoin yarn and patt to end of row.
Now complete to match first side of neck, reversing all shaping.

SLEEVES

Using 3¾ mm needles and A, cast on 35(41) sts.
Work 5 cm in rib as given for back, ending with rib row 1.
Inc row: Rib 4(7), ✳ M1, rib 3, rep from ✳ to last 4(7) sts, M1, rib to end: 45(51) sts.
Change to 3¼ mm needles.
Beg K row and increasing 1 st each end of 3rd row, work 4 rows st st: 47(53) sts.
Now place motifs as follows:
Next row: K11(14)A, working from chart [K10A, 5C, 10A], then K11(14)A.
Increasing 1 st each end of next and every following 3rd row, continue to work from chart as set until row 22 has been completed: 61(67) sts.
Now place 2nd and 3rd motifs as follows:
Next row: Inc in first st, patt as given for last 13(16) sts of first row of chart, K4A, patt across next 25 sts from row 23 of chart, K4A, patt as given for first 13(16) sts of first row of chart, then inc in last st: 63(69) sts.
Continuing to inc each end of every following 3rd row as before, work motifs from chart as set until row 38 of first motif has been completed, then continue with 2nd and 3rd motifs for a further 6 rows: 77(83) sts.
Place 4th motif as follows:
Next row: Patt across first 22(25) sts, K4A, working from chart [K10A, 5C, 10A], K4A, patt across last 22(25) sts.
Continue as set, increasing every 3rd row as before until there are 85(91) sts.
Work straight until row 38 of the 2nd and 3rd motifs has been completed.
2nd size only
Work a further 12 rows straight.
Both sizes
Cast off.

NECKBAND

Join right shoulder seam.
With right side facing and using 2¾ mm needles and A, pick up and K20 sts down left side of front neck, K across 17(21) sts from front neck holder, pick up and K20 sts up right side of front neck, then K across 33(37) sts from back neck holder: 90(98) sts.
Work 2·5 cm in K1, P1 rib.
Cast off in rib.

TO MAKE UP

Join left shoulder seam, leaving 8 cm open at neck edge.
Placing centre of top of sleeves to shoulder seam, sew in sleeves.
Join side and sleeve seams. Make 3 button loops on front edge of shoulder opening, then sew on buttons to correspond.
Press lightly according to instructions on ball band.

36 (40) cm

32 (34·5) cm

23 (26) cm

MUCKY PUP!

Teddy bear bibs for baby and bear!

MATERIALS
Child's bib or Teddy's bib
1 × 50 g ball Phildar Perle No 5 in main colour A
Oddment of yarn for Teddy motif in contrast colour B
Oddment of black for embroidered features
A pair of 3¾ mm (No 9) double-pointed knitting needles for child's bib
A pair of 2¾ mm (No 12) double-pointed knitting needles for Teddy's bib

TENSION
24 sts and 36 rows to 10 cm measured over moss st worked on 3¾ mm needles using yarn double
30 sts and 48 rows to 10 cm measured over moss st worked on 2¾ mm needles using yarn single

NOTES
Instructions given are for teddy's bib, the instructions for the child's bib are given in () brackets. The teddy's bib is worked throughout using the yarn single and the child's bib is worked throughout using the yarn double.

INSTRUCTIONS

TO MAKE
Using 2¾ mm (3¾ mm) needles and 1(2) strands of A, cast on 23 sts.
Row 1: K twice into first st, [P1, K1] to last 2 sts, P twice into next st, K1: 25 sts.
Row 2: K twice into first st, [K1, P1] to last 2 sts, P twice into next st, K1: 27 sts.
Rep these 2 rows 3 times more: 39 sts.
Work 16 rows straight in moss st.
Now work from chart on page 94 as follows:
Row 1: Moss st 7, K25, moss st 7.
Row 2: Moss st 7, P25, moss st 7.
Row 3: Moss st 7A, K4A, 5B, 7A, 5B, 4A, moss st 7A.
Row 4: Moss st 7A, P3A, 7B, 5A, 7B, 3A, moss st 7A.
Working 7 sts in moss st at each end of the rows, continue in patt from chart, working single motif only, until row 25 has been completed. Using A only, work 6 rows st st.
Work 10 rows moss st across all sts, so ending right-side row.
Shape neck
Next row: Moss st 14, cast off 11 sts, moss st to end.
Working on first 14 sts only, dec 1 st at neck edge on next 5 rows: 9 sts.
Work 5 rows moss st.
Shape shoulder
Next row: Cast off 5 sts, K to end.
Next row: P to end: 4 sts.

Now continue in tubular kntting as follows: K1 row.
★ Slide the sts to the other end of the needle, then bringing the yarn across the back of the work and pulling it fairly tightly, K the 4 sts again. ★
Rep from ★ to ★ until tubular piece of knitting measures approximately 23(25·5) cm. Cast off.
Return to remaining sts.
With right side facing, join yarn to remaining sts and complete to match first side of neck, reversing all shaping and working 1 extra row before shaping shoulder.

TO MAKE UP
Darn in all ends neatly, gathering tops of ties to close.
Press lightly on wrong side, following instructions on ball band.

Whether it's porridge on the menu or not, a bib is a must when you're learning to feed yourself! The bear on this bib is knitted or Swiss-darned on a plain knit panel in the midst of a moss stitch surround. And there's a smaller version for Teddy, too (see page 97).

INSIDE OUT

A warm hooded jacket with turn-back cuffs and an easy front fastening.

MEASUREMENTS

To fit chest 41(46,51,56) cm [16(18,20,22) in]
Actual measurements 54(58,64,68) cm
Length to shoulders 28·5(30·5,33·5, 35·5) cm
Sleeve seam 18(20,23,25·5) cm

MATERIALS

1 × 350 g cone Rowan Yarns 3 ply in colour A
3(3,4,4) × 50 g balls Phildar Anouchka in colour B
A pair of 3 mm (No 11) knitting needles

TENSION

29 sts and 40 rows to 10 cm measured over st st worked on 3 mm needles with 3 ply
29 sts and 36 rows to 10 cm measured over st st worked on 3 mm needles with Anouchka

INSTRUCTION

OUTER JACKET BACK

Using 3 mm needles and A, cast on 79(85,93,99) sts.
Beg with a K row, work in st st until back measures 15(15,16·5,18) cm from beg, ending with a P row.
Place a marker each end of last row to denote beg of armholes.
Continue in st st until back measures 27(29,32,34) cm from beg, ending with a P row.
Shape back neck
Next row: K20(22,24,26), K2 tog, turn and leave remaining sts on a spare needle.
Dec 1 st at neck edge on every row until 16(18,20,22) sts remain.
Cast off.
Return to remaining sts.
With right side facing, slip first 35(37,41,43) sts onto a holder, rejoin yarn then K2 tog, K to end.
Now complete to match first side of neck, reversing all shaping.

INNER JACKET BACK

Using B, work as given for outer jacket back.

OUTER JACKET RIGHT FRONT

Using 3 mm needles and A, cast on 59(63,69,73) sts.
Work in st st until front measures same as back to armholes, ending with a P row.
Place a marker at beg of last row to denote beg of armhole.
Continue in st st until front measures 5 cm less than back to shoulder, ending with a P row.
Shape neck
Cast off 24(26,28,30) sts, work until there are

7(7,9,9) sts on needle then slip these sts onto a safety-pin, work 2 tog, work to end.
Dec 1st at neck edge on every row until 16(18,20,22) sts remain.
Work straight until front measures same as back to shoulders.
Cast off.

INNER JACKET RIGHT FRONT

Using B, work as given for outer jacket right front.

OUTER JACKET LEFT FRONT

Work as given for outer jacket right front except end with a K row before placing armhole marker or shaping neck.

INNER JACKET LEFT FRONT

Using B, work as given for outer jacket right front except end with a K row before placing armhole marker or shaping neck.

SLEEVES

Using 3 mm needles and A, cast on 73(87,93,101) sts for top of sleeve.
Beg with a K row, work 8(6,14,24) rows in st st.
Dec 1 st each end of next and every following 4th row until 51(59,65,73) sts remain.
Work straight until sleeve measures 18(20,23, 25·5) cm, ending with a K row.
K1 row to form ridge on right side.
Break off A and join on B.
Continue in st st for 5 cm.
Inc 1 st each end of next and every following 4th row until there are 73(87,93,101) sts.
Work straight until inner sleeve lining measures the same as outer sleeve when sleeve is folded along garter st ridge.
Cast off.

OUTER JACKET HOOD

Join shoulder seams of outer and inner jacket.
With right side of outer jacket facing, slip 7(7,9,9) sts from safety-pin at right front onto a needle, join on A and cast on 8(8,10,10) sts, then K the 7(7,9,9) sts, pick up and K20 sts up right side of front neck, 6 sts down right back neck, decreasing 1 st at centre K across 35(37,41,43) sts from back neck holder, pick up and K6 sts up left side of back neck and 20 sts down left side of front neck, then K across 7(7,9,9) sts from safety-pin at left front neck.
Next row: Cast on 8(8,10,10) sts, P these sts, then P to end: 116(118,130,132) sts.
Continue in st st until hood measures 16(17,18,20) cm from beg, ending with a P row.
Shape crown
Next row: K55(56,62,63), K2 tog, K2, K2 tog tbl, K to end.
Work 3 rows straight.

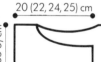
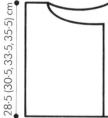

20 (22, 24, 25) cm

28·5 (30·5, 33·5, 35·5) cm

27 (29, 32, 34) cm

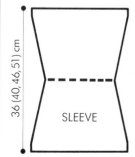

36 (40, 46, 51) cm

SLEEVE

Next row: K54(55,61,62), K2 tog, K2, K2 tog tbl, K to end.
Work 3 rows straight.
Continue decreasing in this way, working 1 st less each side on every 4th row, until 102(102,112,114) sts remain.
Work 1 row straight.
Now either divide the remaining sts onto 2 needles for grafting together or cast off.

INNER JACKET HOOD
Work as given for outer jacket hood.

TO MAKE UP
Join top seams on outer and inner hood. Sew in sleeves between markers, then join side and sleeve seams first on outer and then on inner jacket. Pull sleeve linings into place inside outer jacket sleeves. Join outer jacket edges to lining along fronts and around hood, then finally join jacket to lining all along lower edges.
Make 2 button loops in A on right front edge and 2 button loops in B on left front edge. Sew on buttons to correspond. Press lightly following intructions on ball band.

Even though it's knitted in 3-ply, this hooded jacket will keep little ones as warm as toast. It is reversible – and so double thickness – and makes a smart outfit with the Teddy Dungarees on page 106.

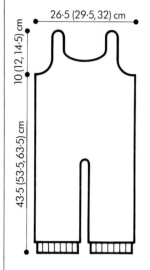

26·5 (29·5, 32) cm

10 (12, 14·5) cm

43·5 (53·5, 63·5) cm

WALKABOUT

Dungarees with a sitting bear motif on the front.

MEASUREMENTS
To fit chest 41–46(51,56) cm [16–18(20,22) in]
Actual measurements 53(59,64) cm
Length from armhole to ankle 43·5(53·5,63·5) cm

MATERIALS
1 × 350 g cone Rowan Yarns 4 ply
Oddment in contrasting yarn for motif
A pair of 3 mm (No 11) knitting needles and one
3 mm (No 11) circular needle
2 buttons

TENSION
29 sts and 40 rows to 10 cm measured over st st
worked on 3 mm needles

INSTRUCTIONS

RIGHT LEG
★ Using the 3 mm needles cast on 39(43,47) sts.
Rib row 1: K2, ✶ P1, K1, rep from ✶ to last st, K1.
Rib row 2: K1, P1, K1, rep from ✶ to end.
Rep these 2 rows for 5(5,7·5) cm, ending with
rib row 2.
Make hem as follows:
Next row: K1, then folding ribbing in half to wrong
side, pick up first loop from cast-on edge and place
onto left-hand needle, then K the loop, K1, ✶ pick up
next loop from cast-on edge and place onto left-
hand needle, K the loop then K1, rep from ✶ to end:
78(86,94) sts.
P1 row.
Beg K row, work in st st until leg measures
23(28,33) cm from lower edge of hem, ending with a
P row. ★
Break off yarn and leave sts on a spare needle.

LEFT LEG
Work as given for right leg from ★ to ★ .
Change to circular needle.
First round: K39(43,47), place a loop of coloured
yarn on needle to denote left side edge, K to last st
of left leg, K tog last st of left leg with first st of right
leg, K38(42,46), place a loop of coloured yarn on
needle to denote right side edge, K to last st of right
leg, place a coloured loop of yarn on needle to
denote centre back then K tog last st of right leg with
first st of left leg: 154(170,186) sts.
Slipping coloured loops on every row, continue in
st st until work measures 19(24,29) cm from crutch,
ending at centre back marker.
Break off yarn and slip first 39(43,47) sts up to
marker onto a holder.

Divide for back and front
Using the pair of 3 mm needles work across the first
77(85,93) sts for front as follows:
Next row: K1, ✶ P1, K1, rep from ✶ to next marker,
turn and leave remaining sts on a holder.
Moss st row: K1, ✶ P1, K1, rep from ✶ to end.
Rep this row 4 times more.
Shape armholes
Cast off 6(6,8) sts at beg of next 2 rows:
65(73,77) sts.
Keeping patt correct, dec 1 st each end of every row
until 49(53,57) sts remain.
Work straight until bib measures 4(5,5) cm from beg
of armhole shaping, ending with a right-side row.
Shape neck
Next row: Moss st 19, cast off 11(15,19), moss st to
end.
Working on first set off sts only, dec 1 st at neck edge
on next 10 rows: 9 sts.
Work straight until strap measures 4(5,7·5) cm from
beg of neck shaping, ending with a wrong-side row.
Place buttonhole
Row 1: [K1,P1] twice, wind yarn twice round needle,
skpo, K1, P1, K1].
Row 2: [K1, P1] twice, K once into large loop, [P1,
K1] twice.
Work 4 rows moss st.
★★ Dec 1 st each end of next and following alternate
row: 5 sts. Cast off. ★★
Return to remaining sts.
With right side facing, rejoin yarn and complete 2nd
side of neck to match first, reversing all shaping.
Now return to remaining sts for back.
With right side facing, rejoin yarn and work in moss
st across all 77(85,93) sts.
Work 5 more rows moss st.
Now complete as given for front bib, except work in
moss st until straps are 8(10,15) cm long, then
omitting buttonholes, shape top as given from
★★ to ★★ .

POCKET (optional)
Using 3 mm needles cast on 35 sts.
Work 6 rows moss st.
Next row: (Right side) Moss st 5, K25, moss st 5.
Next row: Moss st 5, P25, moss st 5.
Rep these 2 rows 14 times more, then the first row
again.
Work 6 rows moss st over all sts, so ending with a
right-side row. Cast off knitwise.

TO MAKE UP
Join inside leg seams, and short underarm seam.
Swiss darn Teddy motif from page 94 either on
pocket or front of dungarees as shown. Sew on
pocket if required. Sew on buttons and neaten
buttonholes. Press lightly following instructions on
ball band.

The pocket on the chest
of these dungarees is
popular with toddlers but for
smaller babies it can be omitted
and the bear motif placed directly
on the front of the dungarees.

CROSS COUNTRY

A long-sleeved jumper in warm DK with a cross-over roll neck.

MEASUREMENTS
To fit chest 46(51,56) cm [18(20,22) in]
Actual measurements 56(61,66) cm
Length to shoulders 28(30·5,33) cm
Sleeve seam 18(20,33) cm

MATERIALS
3(4,4) × 50 g balls King Cole Superwash DK in main colour A
1 ball each of same in contrast colours B, C and D
A pair each of 3¼ mm (No 10) and 4 mm (No 8) knitting needles and one 3¼ mm (No 10) circular needle

TENSION
24 sts and 52 rows to 10 cm measured over pattern worked on 4 mm needles

INSTRUCTIONS

BACK
★ Using 3¼ mm needles and A, cast on 65(71,77) sts.
Rib row 1: K1, ★ P1, K1, rep from ★ to end.
Rib row 2: K2, ★ P1, K1, rep from ★ to last st, K1.
Rep these 2 rows for 4 cm, ending with rib row 1.
Increasing 1 st each end, K1 row: 67(73,79) sts.
Change to 4 mm needles.
Joining on and cutting off colours as required, proceed in patt as follows:
Row 1: With B, K1, ★ sl 1 pw, K1, rep from ★ to end.
Row 2: With B, K1, ★ ytf, sl 1 pw, ytb, K1, rep from ★ to end.
Rows 3 and 4: With A, K to end.
Row 5: With C, K2, ★ sl 1 pw, K1, rep from ★ to last st, K1.
Row 6: With C, K2, ★ ytf, sl 1 pw, ytb, K1, rep from ★ to last st, K1.
Rows 7 and 8: With A, K to end.
Rows 9 and 10: With D, as rows 1 and 2.
Rows 11 and 12: With A, K to end.
Rows 13 and 14: With B, as rows 5 and 6.
Rows 15 and 16: With A, K to end.
Rows 17 and 18: With C, as rows 1 and 2.
Rows 19 and 20: With A, K to end.
Rows 21 and 22: With D, as rows 5 and 6.
Rows 23 and 24: With A, K to end.
These 24 rows form the patt.
Continue in patt until back measures 15(18,19) cm from beg, ending with a wrong-side row in A.
Place a marker each end of last row to denote beg of armholes. ★

Continue in patt until back measures 28(30·5,33) cm from beg, ending with a right-side row in A.
Next row: Cast off 18(21,24), K to end.
Next row: Cast off 18(21,24), then slip remaining 31 sts onto a holder.

FRONT
Work as given for back from ★ to ★.
Continue in patt until front measures 18(20·5,23) cm from beg, ending with a right-side row in A.
Divide for neck
Next row: K18(21,24), cast off next 31 sts, K to end.
Work straight on first set of sts until front measures same as back to shoulders, ending with a wrong-side row in A.
Cast off.
Return to remaining sts.
With right side facing, rejoin yarn and patt to end.
Now complete to match first side of neck.

SLEEVES
Using 3¼ mm needles and A, cast on 37(39,41) sts.
Work 4 cm in rib as given on back, ending rib row 1.
Increasing 1 st each end, K1 row: 39(41,43) sts.
Change to 4 mm needles.
Work in patt as given for back, increasing and working into patt 1 st each end of 5th and every following 4th(4th,6th) row until there are 63(63,69) sts.
Work straight until sleeve measures 18(20,23) cm from beg, ending with a wrong-side row in A.
Using A, cast off.

COLLAR
Join shoulder seams.
With right side facing, using circular needle and A, pick up and K38 sts up right side of front neck, K across 31 sts from back neck holder, then pick up and K38 sts down left side of front neck: 107 sts.
K1 row.
Beg with rib row 1 and working backwards and forwards in rows, work in rib as given for back for 13 cm, ending with rib row 2.
Cast off knitwise.

TO MAKE UP
Sew in sleeves between markers, then join side and sleeve seams. Sew down row ends of collar, lapping left over right for a boy and right over left for a girl.

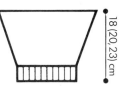

 Warm enough for a cross-country trek, this sweater is easy to get in and out of because of the generous cross-over neck opening. The unusual spot effect is achieved by slip-stitching the main colour every two rows.

28 (30·5, 33) cm

28 (30·5, 33) cm

18 (20, 23) cm

CHRISTMAS STOCKING

Just like a real Christmas stocking, this chapter is bursting with good things! The designs have been deliberately created in bright, festive colours and in warm woollen yarns to keep out the cold. The patterns include a classic party dress, a snowy Fair Isle and a cosy hat and scarf set. And there are motifs for Christmas trees, snowmen, reindeer and a star.

NOËL NOËL

A classic lacy dress with short-sleeves, full skirt and front button fastening.

MEASUREMENTS
To fit chest 51(56) cm [20(22) in]
Actual measurements 54(59) cm
Length to shoulders 44(49) cm
Sleeve seam 2 cm

MATERIALS
5(6) × 50 g balls Patons Promise D.K.
3 buttons
1 metre wide ribbon for sash
A pair of 4 mm (No 8) knitting needles

TENSION
22 sts and 30 rows to 10 cm measured over patt
worked on 4 mm needles

INSTRUCTIONS

Party dresses have to be special and these will certainly not disappoint; little girls love the lacy texture and the full skirts. The effect is completed with satin petticoats, ribbon sashes and ballet slippers.

FRONT
★ Using 4 mm needles cast on 113(119) sts.
Work in patt as follows:
Row 1: K2(5), ✲ yrn, K2 tog, K10, rep from ✲ to last 3(6) sts, yrn, K2 tog, K1(4).
Row 2 and every alternate row: P to end.
Row 3: K3(6), ✲ yrn, K2 tog, K7, skpo, yrn, K1, rep from ✲ to last 2(5) sts, K2(5).

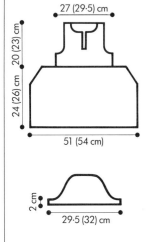

27 (29·5) cm

20 (23) cm

24 (26) cm

51 (54 cm)

2 cm

29·5 (32) cm

Row 5: K3(6), ✶ K1, yrn, K2 tog, K5, skpo, yrn, K2, rep from ✶ to last 2(5) sts, K2(5).
Row 7: As row 3.
Row 9: As row 3.
Row 11: K to end.
Row 13: K to end.
Row 15: K8(11), ✶ yrn, K2 tog, K10, rep from ✶ to last 9(12) sts, yrn, K2 tog, K7(10).
Row 17: K6(9), ✶ skpo, yrn, K1, yrn, K2 tog, K7, rep from ✶ to last 11(14) sts, skpo, yrn, K1, yrn, K2 tog, K6(9).
Row 19: K5(8), ✶ skpo, yrn, K3, yrn, K2 tog, K5, **for 1st size only** rep from ✶ to end, **for 2nd size only** rep from ✶ to last 3 sts, K3.
Row 21: As row 17.
Row 23: As row 17.
Row 25: K to end.
Row 27: K to end.
Row 28: P to end.
These 28 rows form the patt.
Continue in patt until work measures 20(22) cm from beg, ending with a 4th or 18th row of patt.
Side shaping
Keeping patt correct, dec 1 st each end of next 12 rows: 89(95) sts.
Shape for waist
Dec row: For 2nd size only K3, **for both sizes** ✶ K2 tog, K1, rep from ✶ to last 2 sts, **for 1st size only** K2 tog, **for 2nd size only** K2: 59(65) sts. P 1 row.
Place a marker at each end of last row to denote waist.
Working in patt as given for 2nd(1st) size, continue without shaping until work measures 6(7) cm from markers, ending with a wrong-side row.
Shape armholes
Cast off 4 sts at beg of next 2 rows.
Keeping patt correct, dec 1 st each end of next 4 rows: 43(49) sts. ✶
Divide for front neck opening
Next row: Patt 22(25), turn and leave remaining sts on a spare needle.
Work straight in patt until work measures 16(18) cm from markers, ending with a right-side row.
Shape neck
Cast off 11 sts at beg of next row: Dec 1 st at neck edge on next 3 rows: 8(11) sts.
Continue without shaping until work measures 20(23) cm from markers, ending with a wrong-side row.
Cast off.
Return to remaining sts.
With right side facing, join on yarn and patt to end of row: 21(24) sts.
Continue in patt without shaping until work measures 16(18) cm from markers, ending with a wrong-side row.
Shape neck
Cast off 10 sts at beg of next row.

Dec 1 st at neck edge on next 3 rows: 8(11) sts.
Now complete to match first side of neck.

BACK
Work as given for front from ✶ to ✶.
Continue without shaping until work measures 20(23) cm from markers, ending with a wrong-side row.
Cast off 8(11) sts at beg of next 2 rows.
Cast off remaining 27 sts.

SLEEVES
With 4 mm needles cast on 65(71) sts.
Work in patt as given for back for 2 cm.
Shape top
Cast off 4 sts at beg of next 2 rows.
Keeping patt correct, dec 1 st each end of next 4 rows, then at each end of every alternate row until 41(47) sts remain.
Now dec 1 st each end of every row until 13(17) sts remain.
Cast off.

PICOT HEM
With right side facing and using 4 mm needles, pick up and K113(119) sts along lower edge of back.
P 1 row.
Picot edge: Cast off 2 sts, ✶ slip st from right-hand needle back onto left-hand needle, cast on 2 sts, then cast off 4 sts, rep from ✶ to end.
Rep along lower edge of front.

SLEEVE EDGINGS
Work as given for picot hem, picking up 65(71) sts along lower edge of sleeve.

NECKBAND
Join shoulder seams.
With right side facing and using 4 mm needles, pick up and K83 sts evenly round neck edge.
Complete as given for picot hem.

TO MAKE UP
Sew in sleeves, easing in fullness to fit. Join side and sleeve seams. Make 3 buttonloops down right front edge. Sew on buttons to left front to correspond. Make 2 large loops on waist at side seam, then thread sash through. Press lightly following instructions on ball band.

"Christmas is coming
  The goose is getting fat,
Please put a penny
  In the old man's hat.
If you haven't got a penny
  A ha'penny will do,
If you haven't got a ha'penny,
  Then God bless you."

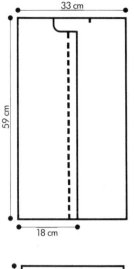

33 cm

59 cm

18 cm

18 cm

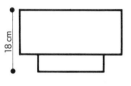

□ =A ● =B

14

10

5

STAR BRIGHT

A warm, hooded baby's sleeping bag with a sparkling Christmas star motif.

MEASUREMENTS
To fit chest 41–46 cm [16–18 in]
Actual measurement 66 cm
Length 59 cm
Sleeve seam 18 cm

MATERIALS
350g Rowan Lightweight D.K.
Oddment of Twilleys Goldfingering for embroidered star motif
8 buttons
A pair each of 3¼ mm (No 10) and 4 mm (No 8) knitting needles

TENSION
24 sts and 48 rows to 10 cm measured over pattern using 4 mm needles

INSTRUCTIONS

BACK
Using 3¼ mm needles cast on 81 sts.
K 3 rows.
Change to 4 mm needles.
Work in patt as follows:
Row 1: K2, * sl 1, K1, rep from * to last st, K1.
Row 2: K2, * ytf, sl 1, ytb, K1, rep from * to last st, K1.
Rows 3 and 4: K to end.
These 4 rows form the patt.
Continue in patt until back measures 59 cm from beg, or length required, ending with row 2 of patt.
Cast off 27 sts at beg of next 2 rows.
Break off yarn and leave remaining 27 sts on a holder.

LEFT FRONT
Using 3¼ mm needles cast on 44 sts.
K 3 rows.
Change to 4 mm needles.
Work in patt with moss st border as follows:
Row 1: K2, * sl 1, K1, rep from * to last 6 sts, [P1, K1] twice, P1, sl 1.
Row 2: [K1, P1] 3 times, K1, * ytf, sl 1, ytb, K1, rep from * to last st, K1.
Row 3: K to last 6 sts, [P1, K1] twice, P1, sl 1.
Row 4: [K1, P1] 3 times, K to end.
These 4 rows form the patt with moss st border.
Continue in patt until front measures 46 cm from beg, ending with row 2 of patt.
Place st st square
Next row: (Right side) K to last 6 sts, moss st 6.
Next row: Moss st 6, K7, P17, K14.

Next row: Patt 14, K17, patt 7, moss st 6.
Next row: Moss st 6, patt 7, P17, patt 14.
Rep these last 4 rows three times more, then the first 2 rows again.
Continue in patt with moss st border across all sts until front measures 20 rows less than back to shoulders.
Shape neck
Next row: Patt to last 6 sts, moss st 6.
Next row: Cast off 6 sts purlwise, patt to end: 38 sts.
Next row: Patt to last 6 sts, K2 tog, K1, turn and leave remaining 3 sts on a safety-pin.
Keeping patt correct, dec 1 st at neck edge on every row until 27 sts remain.
Work straight until front measures same as back to shoulder.
Cast off.
Mark positions on moss st border for 8 buttons, the first one 7·5 cm from lower edge, the top one 2 cm from neck edge and the others spaced evenly in between.

RIGHT FRONT
Using 3¼ mm needles cast on 44 sts.
K 3 rows.
Change to 4 mm needles.
Work in patt with moss st border as follows:
Row 1: (Right side) [K1, P1] 3 times, * K1, sl 1, rep from * to last 2 sts, K2.
Row 2: K2, * ytf, sl 1, ytb, K1, rep from * to last 6 sts, [P1, K1] twice, P1, sl 1.
Row 3: [K1, P1] 3 times, K to end.
Row 4: K to last 6 sts, [P1, K1] twice, P1, sl 1.
These 4 rows form patt with moss st border.
Continue in patt until front measures 20 rows less than back to shoulders and AT THE SAME TIME work buttonholes to correspond with markers as follows:
Buttonhole row: (Right side) K1, P1, K1, yrn, skpo, P1, patt to end.
Shape neck
Next row: Cast off 6 sts, patt to end.
Next row: Patt to last 3 sts, turn and leave remaining 3 sts on a safety-pin.
Now complete to match left front, reversing all shaping.

SLEEVES
Using 3¼ mm needles cast on 37 sts.
Rib row 1: K2, * P1, K1, rep from * to last st, K1.
Rib row 2: K1, * P1, K1, rep from * to end.
Rep these 2 rows for 5 cm, ending rib row 2.
Change to 4 mm needles.
Inc row: K into front and back of every st: 74 sts.
Next row: K to end, inc in last st: 75 sts.
Now work in patt as given for back until sleeve measures 18 cm from beg, ending with a row 4 of patt. Cast off.

NECKBAND AND HOOD

Join shoulder seams.

With right side facing and using 3¼ mm needles, join on yarn at right front neck edge and K3 sts from safety-pin, pick up and K19 sts up right side of neck, K across 27 sts from back neck holder, pick up and K19 sts down left front neck, then K3 sts from safety-pin: 71 sts.

Beg rib row 2, work 3 rows rib.

Change to 4 mm needles.

Inc row: Rib 8, [inc in next st, rib 7] 7 times, inc in next st, rib to end: 79 sts.

Next row: K to end.

Now work in patt as given for back until hood measures 13 cm from beg, ending with row 2 of patt.

Shape crown

Row 1: K37, K2 tog, K1, K2 tog tbl, K to end.

Patt 3 rows.

Row 5: K36, K2 tog, K1, K2 tog tbl, K to end.

Patt 3 rows.

Continue decreasing each side of centre st on next and every following 4th row until 67 sts remain.

Patt 1 row, so ending with a wrong-side row.

Cast off purlwise.

TO MAKE UP

Join seam at top of hood.

Border: With right side facing and using 3¼ mm needles, pick up and K81 sts evenly round edge of hood.

K 1 row.

Change to 4 mm needles and cast off purlwise. Sew in sleeves, then join side and sleeve seams. Neaten buttonholes and sew on buttons. Using 2 strands of lurex, Swiss darn star motif onto st st square at top of left front. Join lower edge of sleeping bag if required, lapping buttonhole border over button border.

This roomy baby's sleeping bag is knitted in lightweight double knitting which makes it warm without being bulky. By the time he or she is standing, the bottom can be unpicked and, hey presto, you will have a little hooded dressing gown.

CHRISTMAS CRACKER

A smart V-neck slipover to wear with a shirt or blouse, complete with matching bow tie.

MEASUREMENTS
Child's slipover
To fit chest 46(51,56) cm [18(20,22) in]
Actual measurements 55(58,62) cm
Length to shoulders 28(30·5,33) cm
Teddy's slipover
To fit chest 38 cm [15 in]

MATERIALS
Child's slipover
1(1,2) × 50 g balls Schaffhauser Lambswool (3 ply) in main colour A
Teddy's slipover
1 ball same in main colour A
Both slipovers
1 × 25 g ball Twilleys Goldfingering in contrast colour B
A pair each of 2¼ mm (No 13) and 3¼ mm (No 10) knitting needles
Bow Tie
Small amount of contrast colour B
A pair of 2¾ mm (No 12) knitting needles
3·00 mm crochet hook

TENSION
32 sts and 40 rows to 10 cm measured over st st worked on 3¼ mm needles

INSTRUCTIONS FOR CHILD'S SLIPOVER

FRONT
★ Using 2¼ mm needles and A, cast on 85(91,97) sts.
Rib row 1: K2, ★ P1, K1, rep from ★ to last st, K1.
Rib row 2: K1, ★ P1, K1, rep from ★ to end.
Rep these 2 rows for 2·5(4,4) cm, ending rib row 2.
Change to 3¼ mm needles.
Inc row: K21(24,27), ★ inc in next st, K20, rep from ★ once more, inc in next st, K21(24,27): 88(94,100) sts.
P 1 row. ★
Work in Square patt as follows:
Row 1: K1B, ★ 2A, 4B, rep from ★ to last 3 sts, K2A, 1B.
Row 2: P1B, ★ 2A, 4B, rep from ★ to last 3 sts, P2A, 1B.
Rows 3 and 4: As rows 1 and 2.
Row 5: K with A.
Row 6: P with A.
These 6 rows form the patt.
Continue in patt until front measures 14(16·5,19) cm from beg, ending with a wrong-side row.
Shape armholes
Cast off 4 sts at beg of next 2 rows: 80(86,92) sts.

Divide for neck
Keeping patt correct, K2 tog, patt next 38(41,44) sts, turn and leave remaining sts on a spare needle.
Dec 1 st at armhole edge on the next 8 rows, then on the following 3 alternate rows AT THE SAME TIME dec 1 st at neck edge on the 2nd and every following alternate row until 8(11,14) sts remain.
Work straight until front measures 28(30·5,33) cm from beg, ending with row 6 of patt.
Cast off.
Return to remaining sts.
With right side facing, join on yarns and patt to last 2 sts, K2 tog: 39(42,45) sts.
Now complete to match first side of neck, reversing all shaping.

BACK
Work as given for front from ★ to ★ .
Using A only, continue in st st until back measures same as front to armholes, ending with P row.
Shape armholes
Cast off 4 sts at beg of next 2 rows.
Dec 1 st each end of next 9 rows: 62(68,74) sts.
Now dec 1 st each end of following 3 alternate rows: 56(62,68) sts.
Work straight until back measures 4 rows less than front, ending with a P row.
Shape neck
Next row: K10(13,16), K2 tog, turn and leave remaining sts on a spare needle.
Dec 1 st at neck edge on next 3 rows.
Cast off.
Return to remaining sts.
With right side facing, slip first 32 sts onto a holder, join on yarn, K2 tog, K to end.
Now complete to match first side of neck, reversing all shaping.

NECKBAND
Join left shoulder seam.
With right side facing and using 2¼ mm needles and A, pick up and K53 sts down right side of front neck.
Work 7 rows in rib as given for back.
Cast off.
With right side facing and using 2¼ mm needles and A, pick up and K4 sts down right side of back neck, K across 32 sts on back neck holder, pick up and K4 sts up left side of back neck and 53 sts down left side of front neck: 93 sts.
Work 7 rows in rib as given for back.
Cast off.

ARMHOLE BORDERS
Join right shoulder and neckband seam.
With right side facing and using 2¼ mm needles and A, pick up and K103 sts evenly round armhole edge.
Work 7 rows in rib as given for back.
Cast off.

Glittery gold yarn turns these smart little slip-overs for children and Teddy into something very special indeed for Christmas parties.

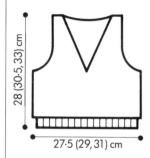

28 (30·5, 33) cm

27·5 (29, 31) cm

TO MAKE UP

Crossing left over right for a boy or right over left for a girl, stitch front neckband edges into place. Join side and armhole border seams. Press lightly following instructions on ball band.

INSTRUCTIONS FOR TEDDY'S SLIPOVER

FRONT

★★ Using 2¼ mm needles and A, cast on 69 sts.
Work in rib as given for front of child's slipover for 8 rows.
Change to 3¼ mm needles.
Work 2 rows st st, increasing 1 st at beg of first row: 70 sts. ★★
Now work in patt as given for front of child's slipover until front measures 9 cm from beg, ending with a wrong-side row.
Place a marker at each end of last row to denote beg of armholes.

Divide for neck
Next row: Patt 33, K2 tog, turn and leave remaining sts on a spare needle.
Keeping patt correct, dec 1 st at neck edge on every following alternate row until 16 sts remain.
Work straight until front measures 19 cm from beg, ending with row 6 of patt.
Cast off.
Return to remaining sts.
With right side facing, join on yarns, K2 tog, patt to end of row.
Now complete to match first side of neck, reversing all shaping.

BACK

Work as given for front from ★★ to ★★ .
Using A only, work in st st until back measures same as front to armhole markers, ending with a P row.
Place a marker at each end of last row.
Continue in st st until back measures 4 rows less than front, ending with a P row.

Shape neck
Next row: K18, K2 tog, turn and leave remaining sts on a spare needle.
Dec 1 st at neck edge on next 3 rows.
Cast off.
Return to remaining sts.
With right side facing, slip first 30 sts onto a holder, join on yarn, K2 tog, K to end.
Now complete to match first side of neck, reversing all shaping.

NECKBAND

Join left shoulder seam.
With right side facing and using 2¼mm needles and A, pick up and K41 sts down right side of front neck.
Work 5 rows in rib as given for back of child's slipover. Now cast off.

With right side facing and using 2¼ mm needles and A, pick up and K4 sts down right side of back neck, K across 30 sts on back neck holder, pick up and K4 sts up left side of back neck and 41 sts down left side of front neck: 79 sts.
Work 5 rows in rib as before. Cast off.

ARMHOLE BORDERS

Join right shoulder and neckband seam.
With right side facing and using 2¼ mm needles and A, pick up and K77 sts evenly between markers.
Complete as for neckband.

TO MAKE UP

Crossing left over right, stitch front neckband edges into place. Join side and armhole border seams. Press lightly following instructions on ball band.

INSTRUCTIONS FOR BOW TIE

Note For the child's bow tie, use the gold yarn double. For Teddy's bow tie, use the gold yarn single.

TO MAKE

Using 2¾ mm (No 12) knitting needles and B, and using the yarn double or single as appropriate, cast on 1 st.
Row 1: K into front and back of st: 2 sts.
Row 2: K into front and back of first st, K1: 3 sts.
Row 3: K into front and back of first st, P1, K into front and back of last st: 5 sts.
Row 4: Inc in first st, K1, P1, K1, inc in last st: 7 sts.
Row 5: K1, [P1, K1] to end.
This last row forms the moss st patt, continue in moss st until work measures 7·5 cm from beg.
Shape centre of bow
Keeping moss st patt correct, dec 1 st each end of next 2 rows: 3 sts.
Now inc 1 st each end of next 2 rows: 7 sts. Continue in moss st until work measures 15 cm from beg.
Shape end
Keeping patt correct, dec 1 st each end of next 2 rows, then 1 st at beg of following 2 rows: 1 st.
Break yarn and fasten off.

CENTRE BAND

Cast on 3 sts.
Moss st row: K1, P1, K1.
Rep this row until band measures 5 cm from beg.
Cast off.

TO MAKE UP

Using crochet hook, crochet a chain approximately 61 cm long. Fold bow by placing cast-on and cast-off points to centre back and stitch to secure. Fold band over centre of bow and stitch at back. Knot crocheted chain over back of band and secure to back of bow with small stitches.

CHRISTMAS TREES

A round-neck, long-sleeved, fuzzy Christmas cardigan decorated all over with bright green fir trees and tiny pearl beads.

MEASUREMENTS
To fit chest 51(56,61) cm [20(22,24) in]
Actual measurements 54(61,69) cm
Length to shoulders 32(35,38) cm
Sleeve seam 20(24,27) cm

MATERIALS
2(3,4)×50 g balls of Berger Du Nord Kid Mohair in main colour
Oddment of Green mohair for embroidered trees
Small pearl beads for decoration
6 pearl buttons
A pair each of 4½ mm (No 7) and 5½ mm (No 5) knitting needles

TENSION
17 sts and 20 rows to 10 cm measured over st st worked on 5½ mm needles

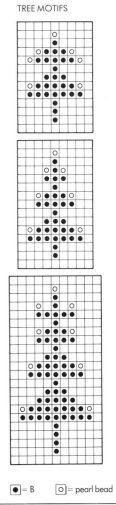

TREE MOTIFS

● = B   ○ = pearl bead

Children adore this special Christmas cardigan because of its soft fluffy texture and because the tree motifs are so clearly recognizable – they even get on to the back (see over page)

The Christmas tree cardigan is seen here from behind; the tree motifs can be placed anywhere you like.

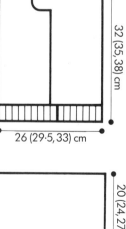

32 (35, 38) cm

26 (29·5, 33) cm

20 (24, 27) cm

INSTRUCTIONS

BACK

Using 4½ mm needles cast on 44(50,56) sts.
Twisted rib row: * K1 tbl, P1, rep from * to end.
Rep this row 9 times more.
Change to 5½ mm needles.
Beg K row, work in st st until back measures 32(35,38) cm from beg, ending with a P row.
Cast off 14(16,18) sts at beg of next 2 rows.
Break off yarn and leave remaining 16(18,20) sts on a holder.

RIGHT FRONT

Using 4½ mm needles cast on 29(32,35) sts.
Work 4 rows in twisted rib as given for back.
Next row: Rib 2, yf, K2 tog, rib to end.
Work 5 more rows in twisted rib.
Next row: Rib 7 and slip these 7 sts onto a safety-pin, change to 5½ mm needles then K to end: 22(25,28) sts.
Beg P row, continue in st st until front measures 10 rows less than back to shoulders ending P row.
Shape neck
Row 1: (Right side) Cast off 3(4,5) sts, work to end.
Row 2: Work to end.
Row 3: Work 2 tog, work to end.
Row 4: Work to last 2 sts, work 2 tog.
Rows 5 and 6: As rows 3 and 4.
Row 7: As row 3.
Row 8: Work to end: 14(16,18) sts.
Work 2 rows straight.
Cast off.

LEFT FRONT

Using 4½ mm needles cast on 29(32,35) sts.
Work 10 rows twisted rib as given for back.
Next row: K to last 7 sts, turn and leave remaining sts on a safety-pin: 22(25,28) sts.
Now complete to match right front, reversing all shaping.

SLEEVES

Using 4½ mm needles cast on 26(26,28) sts.
Work 7 rows twisted rib.
Inc row: Rib 3(3,2), * K into front and back of next st, rep from * to last 3(3,2) sts, rib to end: 46(46,52) sts.
Change to 5½ mm needles.
Beg K row, work in st st until sleeve measures 19(23,26) cm from beg, ending with a P row.
K 5 rows.
Cast off.

NECKBAND

Join shoulder seams.
With right side facing and using 4½ mm needles, join on yarn and pick up and K10 sts up right side of front neck, K16(18,20) sts from back neck holder, then pick up and K10 sts down left side of front neck: 36(38,40) sts.
Work 12 rows in twisted rib.
Cast off loosely in rib.
Fold neckband in half to wrong side and slipstitch into position.

BUTTON BORDER

With right side of left front facing, slip the 7 sts from safety-pin onto a 4½ mm needle, join on yarn then P1, [K1 tbl, P1] 3 times.
Continue in twisted rib until border, slightly stretched fits up left front to top of neckband.
Cast off.
Sew on the border, then mark the positions for the 6 buttons, the first one 1.5 cm from lower edge, the top one 1.5 cm from cast-off edge and the others spaced evenly in between.

BUTTONHOLE BORDER

With wrong side of right front facing, slip the 7 sts from safety-pin onto a 4½ mm needle, join on yarn then P1, [K1 tbl, P1] 3 times
Continue in twisted rib to match button border, working buttonholes to correspond with markers as follows:
Buttonhole row: (Right side) Rib 2, yf, K2 tog, rib 3.

TO MAKE UP

Using green mohair, Swiss darn tree motifs as required. Sew on beads to decorate as required.
Fold sleeves in half lengthwise, then placing folds to shoulder seams, sew into place. Join side and sleeve seams. Sew on buttonhole border. Sew on buttons.

CHRISTMAS WRAPPING

Matching hat, scarf, mittens and ankle-warmers.

MEASUREMENTS

Hat To fit head up to 51 cm in circumference
Scarf Length approximately 116 cm

MATERIALS

6 × 50 g balls King Cole 4 ply in main colour A
Oddments of White angora for snowmen (contrast colour B)
Oddments of Black 4 ply for hats (contrast colour C)
Oddments of Orange for embroidery
A pair each of 2¼ mm (No 13), 2¾ mm (No 12) and 3 mm (No 11) knitting needles

TENSION

32 sts and 40 rows to 10 cm measured over st st worked on 3 mm needles

INSTRUCTIONS FOR HAT

Using 2¼ mm needles and A, cast on 146 sts.
Work in g st for 4·5 cm, ending with a right-side row.
Now continue in rib as follows:
Rib row 1: (Right side) K2, ✲ P2, K2, rep from ✲ to end.
Rib row 2: K1, P1, ✲ K2, P2, rep from ✲ to last 4 sts, K2, P1, K1.
Rep these 2 rows for 3 cm, ending rib row 2 and inc 1 st at end of last row: 147 sts.
Change to 3 mm needles.
Beg K row, work in st st for 2·5 cm, ending with a P row.

This smart set of mittens, hat, scarf and ankle-warmers (see over page) would make a marvellous Christmas present. The Baby's mitts (not shown) are knitted without a thumb to make them as easy as possible to put on.

Joining on colours as required work in patt from chart for snowmen as follows:
Row 1: K4A, [7B, 5A] 11 times, 7B, 4A.
Row 2: P3A, [9B, 3A] 12 times.
Continue in patt from chart until row 22 has been completed.
Using A only, continue in st st until hat measures 15 cm from top of rib, ending with a P row.
Shape crown
Row 1: ✲ K2 tog, rep from ✲ to last st, K1: 74 sts.
K5 rows.
Row 7: ✲ K2 tog, rep from ✲ to end: 37 sts.
K 5 rows.
Row 13: ✲ K2 tog, rep from ✲ to last st, K1: 19 sts.
K 2 rows.
Break off yarn leaving a long length, thread through sts, draw up tightly and secure.

TO MAKE UP

Using black, Swiss darn buttons and eyes on snowmen. Using orange, work a French knot for the nose of each snowman. Join back seam.

INSTRUCTIONS FOR SCARF

Using 2¼ mm needles and A, cast on 75 sts.
K 8 rows.
Change to 3 mm needles.
Beg K row, work 4 cm in st st, ending with a P row.
Joining on colours as required work in patt from chart for snowmen as follows:
Row 1: K5B, [5A, 7B] 5 times, 5A, 5B.
Row 2: P6B, [3A, 9B] 5 times, 3A, 6B.
Continue in patt from chart until row 22 has been completed.
Using A only, continue in st st until scarf measures 104 cm from beg, ending with a P row.

Now turning chart upside down work in patt for snowmen as follows:
Row 1: K4C, [7A, 5C] 5 times, 7A, 4C.
Row 2: P5C, [5A, 7C] 5 times, 5A, 5C.
Continue in patt in this way until all 22 rows of chart have been completed.
Working in A only and beg K row, work 4 cm in st st, ending with a P row.
Change to 2¼ mm needles.
K 8 rows.
Cast off.

TO MAKE UP

Embroider snowmen as given for hat. Join centre back seam of scarf, taking care to match up the two halves of snowmen at each end. Join lower edges. Press lightly following instructions on ball band.

INSTRUCTIONS FOR ANKLE-WARMERS

Using 2¾ mm needles and A, cast on 62 sts.
Work in rib as given for hat for 5 cm, ending rib row 2 and inc 1 st at end of last row: 63 sts.
Change to 3 mm needles.
Beg K row, work 3 cm in st st, ending with a P row.
Joining on colours as required, work in patt from chart for snowmen as follows:
Row 1: K4A, [7B, 5A] 4 times, 7B, 4A.
Row 2: P3A, [9B, 3A] 5 times.
Continue in patt from chart until row 22 has been completed.
Using A only and beg K row, work 4 cm st st, ending with a P row and dec 1 st at end of last row: 62 sts.
Change to 2¾ mm needles.
Rep the 2 rib rows for 3 cm, ending rib row 2.
Work 4 cm in g st.
Cast off.

TO MAKE UP

Embroider snowmen as given for hat. Join seam. Press lightly following instructions on ball band.

INSTRUCTIONS FOR MITTENS

RIGHT MITTEN

✲ Using 2¼ mm needles and A, cast on 46 sts.
K 17 rows.
Work in rib as follows:
Rib row 1: K2, ✲ P2, K2, rep from ✲ to end.
Rib row 2: K1, P1, K2, ✲ P2, K2, rep from ✲ to last 2 sts, P1, K1.
Rep these 2 rows 4 times more.
Change to 3 mm needles.
Inc row: K15, ✲ M1, K15, rep from ✲ to last st, K1: 48 sts. ✲
Beg P row, work 7 rows st st.
Shape thumb gusset
Row 1: K25, M1, K1, M1, K22.
Row 2: P to end.

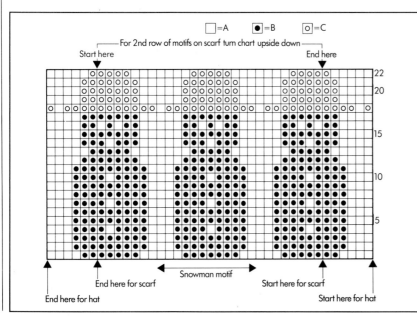

□ =A ●=B ⊙=C

For 2nd row of motifs on scarf turn chart upside down
Start here   End here
22
20
15
10
5
Snowman motif
End here for scarf   Start here for scarf
End here for hat   Start here for hat

Row 3: K25, M1, K3, M1, K22.
Row 4: P to end.
Continue inc 1 st each side of gusset on next and every following alternate row until there are 62 sts. P 1 row.
Next row: K40, turn and cast on 2 sts.
Next row: P16, turn and cast on 2 sts: 18 sts.
Work 2.5 cm in st st on these 18 sts, ending with a P row.
Next row: K1, [K2, K2 tog] 4 times, K1: 14 sts.
Next row: P to end.
Next row: ✻ K2 tog, rep from ✻ to end, break off yarn, thread through sts then draw up tightly and secure. Join seam of thumb.
Return to remaining sts.
Join on yarn at base of thumb and with right-hand needle, pick up and K4 sts from base of thumb, K remaining 22 sts from left-hand needle: 52 sts.
Beg P row, work 4 cm in st st, ending with a P row.
Shape top
Row 1: K2, [skpo, K19, K2 tog, K2] twice.
Row 2 and every alternate row: P to end.
Row 3: K2, [skpo, K17, K2 tog, K2] twice.
Row 5: K2, [skpo, K15, K2 tog, K2] twice.
Row 7: K2, [skpo, K13, K2 tog, K2] twice.
Row 9: K2, [skpo, K11, K2 tog, K2] twice: 32 sts.
Cast off.

TO MAKE UP

Swiss-darn snowman motif onto back of mitten, then embroider as given for hat. Join top and side seam.

LEFT MITTEN

Work as given for right mitten from ✻ to ✻.
Shape thumb gusset
Row 1: K22, M1, K1, M1, K25.
Row 2: P to end.
Row 3: K22, M1, K3, M1, K25.
Row 4: P to end.
Continue inc 1 st each side of gusset on next and every following alternate row until there are 62 sts. P 1 row.
Next row: K36, turn and cast on 2 sts.
Next row: P16, turn and cast on 2 sts: 18 sts.
Work 2·5 cm in st st on these 18 sts, ending with a P row.
Complete as given for thumb of right mitten.
Return to remaining sts.
Join on yarn at base of thumb and with right-hand needle, pick up and K4 sts from base of thumb, K remaining 26 sts from left-hand needle: 52 sts.
Now complete as given for right mitten.

INSTRUCTIONS FOR BABY'S MITTS

(alike)
Using 2¼ mm needles and A, cast on 38 sts.
K 15 rows. Work in rib as follows:
Rib row 1: K2, ✻ P2, K2, rep from ✻ to end.

Rib row 2: K1, P1, K2, ✻ P2, K2, rep from ✻ to last 2 sts, P1, K1.
Rep these 2 rows 3 times more.
Change to 3 mm needles.
Inc row: K6, ✻ M1, K5, rep from ✻ to last 2 sts, K2: 44 sts.
Beg P row, work in st st until mitt measures 10 cm from beg, ending with a P row.
Shape top
Row 1: K2, [skpo, K15, K2 tog, K2] twice: 40 sts.
Row 2 and every alternate row: P to end.
Row 3: K2, [skpo, K13, K2 tog, K2] twice: 36 sts.
Row 5: K2, [skpo, K11, K2 tog, K2] twice: 32 sts.
Row 7: K2, [skpo, K9, K2 tog, K2] twice: 28 sts.
Cast off.

TO MAKE UP

Swiss-darn snowman motif onto back of mitt, then embroider as given for hat. Join top and side seam. Fold back cuff.

Ensure that your toddler's legs are warm in the snowy weather, by bridging the gap between boots and snowsuit with a pair of snug ankle-warmers.

CHRISTMAS STOCKING

A traditional Christmas stocking complete with fir trees and reindeer.

MATERIALS

3 × 50 g balls King Cole Superwash D.K. in main colour A
1 ball each of same in contrast colours B and C
1 × 25 g ball Twilleys Goldfingering in contrast colour D (used double)
A set of four 4 mm (No 8) and 4½ mm (No 7) double-pointed knitting needles

TENSION

24 sts and 30 rows to 10 cm measured over st st worked on 4 mm needles

INSTRUCTIONS

Using 4 mm needles and A, cast on 72 sts and arrange over 3 needles, so placing 24 sts on each needle.
Knit 36 rounds.
Next round: (Picot edge) ✳ yf, skpo, rep from ✳ to end.
Knit a further 40 rounds.
Using the 4½ mm needles for the Fair Isle rows and the 4 mm needles for the st st rows, work in patt from chart, rep the 24 sts patt 3 times in each round, until row 59 has been completed.
Change to 4 mm needles.
Knit 2 rounds.

Shape ankle

Next round: K1, skpo, K to last 3 sts, K2 tog, K1.
Knit 4 rounds.
Rep these last 5 rounds until 58 sts remain.

Shape heel

Break off A.
Re-arrange sts as follows:
Slip last 15 sts of third needle and first 16 of first needle onto fourth needle. (There should now be 31 sts on this needle.)
Divide remaining 27 sts onto remaining 2 needles and leave.
Join on C and work backwards and forwards in rows on 31 sts of first needle only, as follows:
Row 1: K to end.
Row 2: P to end.
Dec 1 st at beg of next 22 rows: 9 sts.
Now inc 1 st at end of next 22 rows by picking up corresponding decreased loop of previous 22 rows: 31 sts. Break off C.
Join on A and working in rounds over all 58 sts, knit 1 round re-arranging sts so that there are 20 sts on first needle and 19 on each of second and third and noting that round now begins at side edge of foot.
Knit 36 rounds. Break off A.
Join on C and knit 6 rounds.

Shape toe

Round 1: [K1, skpo, K23, K2 tog, K1] twice.
Round 2: K to end.
Round 3: [K1, skpo, K21, K2 tog, K1] twice.
Round 4: K to end.
Continue dec in this way on every alternate round until 22 sts remain.
Cast off.

TO MAKE UP

Turn stocking inside out and join toe seam. Fold hem at top of stocking to wrong-side and slipstitch into place. Either by crochet, plaiting or using the tubular knitting technique (see page 88), make a length of cord 20 cm long and stitch to back at top edge of stocking.

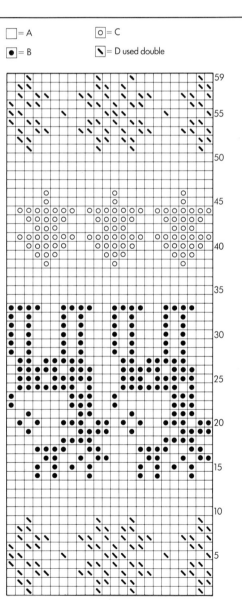

Christmas just wouldn't be Christmas without a stocking piled high with presents and goodies. This one is sturdy and will accommodate the heaviest Christmas deliveries!

AND SO TO BED

A luxurious little raglan dressing gown with a roll-over collar, deep pocket and long, tie belt.

MEASUREMENTS

To fit chest 56 cm [22 in]
Actual measurement 81 cm
Length to shoulders 56 cm
Sleeve seam with cuff turned back 23 cm

MATERIALS

14 × 50 g balls Phildar Skate
A pair of 5 mm (No 6) knitting needles
5·00 mm (No 6) crochet hook

TENSION

17 sts and 24 rows to 10 cm measured over pattern using 5 mm needles and 2 strands of yarn

NOTE

Yarn is used double throughout

INSTRUCTIONS

BACK
Using 5 mm needles and 2 strands of yarn, cast on 73 sts.
K 3 rows.
Work in patt as follows:
Row 1: (Right side) K1, * P1, K1, rep from * to end.
Row 2: P1, * K1, P1, rep from * to end.
Rows 3 and 4: K to end.
These 4 rows form the patt.
Continue in patt until back measures 38 cm from beg, ending with row 2 of patt.
Shape raglan
Cast off 4 sts at beg of next 2 rows.
Next row: K1, skpo, patt to last 3 sts, K2 tog, K1.
Next row: P2, patt to last 2 sts, P2.
Rep these 2 rows until 21 sts remain, ending with a wrong-side row.
Cast off.

LEFT FRONT
★ Using 5 mm needles and 2 strands of yarn, cast on 47 sts.
K 3 rows. ★
Work in patt as follows:
Row 1: * K1, P1, rep from * to last 3 sts, K3.
Row 2: K2, P1, * K1, P1, rep from * to end.
Rows 3 and 4: K to end.
These 4 rows form the patt.
Continue in patt until front measures same as back to beg of raglan shaping, ending with a wrong-side row.
Shape raglan
Cast off 4 sts at beg of next row.
Patt 1 row.
Next row: K1, skpo, patt to end.
Next row: Patt to last 2 sts, P2.
Rep these 2 rows until 21 sts remain, ending with a wrong-side row.
Now work collar as follows:
Row 1: K4, * K1, P1, rep from * to last 3 sts, K3.
Row 2: K2, P1 * K1, P1, rep from * to last 4 sts, K4.
Rows 3 and 4: K to end.
Row 5: As row 1.
Row 6: K2, P1, * K1, P1, rep from * to last 4 sts, turn.
Row 7: Sl 1, K to end.
Row 8: K across all sts.
Rep these 8 rows until shorter edge measures 10 cm.
Cast off.

RIGHT FRONT
Work as given for left front from ★ to ★.
Work in patt as follows:
Row 1: K3, * P1, K1, rep from * to end.
Row 2: * P1, K1, rep from * to last 3 sts, P1, K2.
Rows 3 and 4: K to end.
These 4 rows form the patt.

Continue in patt until front measures same as back to armholes, ending with a right-side row.
Shape raglan
Cast off 4 sts at beg of next row.
Next row: Patt to last 3 sts, K2 tog, K1.
Next row: P2, patt to end.
Rep these 2 rows until 21 sts remain, ending with a wrong-side row.
Now work collar as follows:
Row 1: K3, * P1, K1, rep from * to last 4 sts, K4.
Row 2: K4, * P1, K1, rep from * to last 3 sts, P1, K2.
Rows 3 and 4: K to end.
Rows 5 and 6: As rows 1 and 2.
Row 7: K to last 4 sts, turn.
Row 8: Sl 1, K to end.
Rep these 8 rows until shorter edge measures 10 cm.
Cast off.

SLEEVES
Using 5 mm needles and 2 strands of yarn, cast on 41 sts.
Work in patt as given for back for 5 cm to form cuff.
Continue in patt increasing and working into patt 1 st each end of next and every following 6th row until there are 57 sts.
Work straight until sleeve measures 27 cm from beg, ending with a row 2 of patt.
Cast off 4 sts at beg of next 2 rows. Shape raglan as given for back until 5 sts remain, ending with a wrong-side row. Cast off.

POCKET
Using 5 mm needles and 2 strands of yarn, cast on 19 sts.
Rep the 4 patt rows 4 times, then rows 3 and 4 again.
Cast off.

BELT
Using 5 mm needles and 2 strands of yarn, cast on 9 sts.
K 3 rows.
Work in patt as follows:
Row 1: K3, P1, K1, P1, K3.
Row 2: K2, [P1, K1] twice, P1, K2.
Rows 3 and 4: K to end.
Rep these 4 rows until belt measures approximately 132 cm or length required. Cast off.

BELT LOOPS (make 2)
Using 5·00 mm crochet hook and 2 strands of yarn, make 14 ch then fasten off.

TO MAKE UP
Join raglan seams. Join centre back collar seam, then sew edge of collar to sleeve tops and back neck. Join side and sleeve seams. Sew on pocket. Stitch one belt loop to each side seam. Thread through belt to tie.

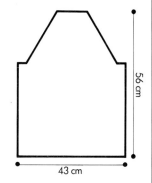

43 cm

56 cm

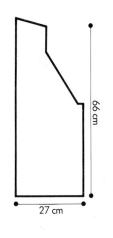

66 cm

27 cm

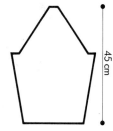

45 cm

A truly grown-up-looking dressing gown which is knitted using the cotton yarn double throughout. This makes it specially soft and warm and very luxurious!

SNOWFLAKES

This long-sleeved snowy sweater sports a Fair Isle design. It also has a slash neck and fastens with two buttons on each shoulder.

MEASUREMENTS

To fit chest 46(51,56) cm [18(20,22) in]
Actual measurements 56(61,66) cm
Length to shoulders 28·5(30,32·5) cm
Sleeve seam 20(23, 25·5) cm

MATERIALS

3 × 50 g balls King Cole Superwash 4 ply in main colour A
1 ball same in contrast colour B
A pair each of 2¼ mm (No 13) and 3 mm (No 11) knitting needles
4 buttons

TENSION

32 sts and 40 rows to 10 cm measured over st st worked on 3 mm needles
32 sts and 36 rows to 10 cm measured over Fair Isle patt worked on 3 mm needles

INSTRUCTIONS

BACK AND FRONT (alike)

Using 2¼ mm needles and A, cast on 87(95,103) sts.
Rib row 1: K2, * P1, K1, rep from * to last st, K1.
Rib row 2: K1, * P1, K1, rep from * to end.
Rep these 2 rows for 2·5 cm.
Change to 3 mm needles.
Inc row: K12(16,20), * inc in next st, K20, rep from * to last 12(16,20) sts, inc in next st, K to end: 91(99,107) sts.
Beg P row, work 3 rows st st.
Joining in B as required, continue in patt as follows:
Row 1: K1A, * 1B, 3A, rep from * to last 2 sts, K1B, 1A.
Row 2: P with A.
Row 3: K with A.
Rows 4 and 5: As rows 2 and 3.
Row 6: P3A, * 1B, 3A, rep from * to end.
Row 7: K with A.
Row 8: P with A.
Rows 9 and 10: As rows 7 and 8.
These 10 rows form Spot patt.
Continue in patt until work measures approximately 15(16·5,19) cm from beg, ending with row 10 of patt.
Now work from chart, working edge sts as indicated until row 44 has been completed.
Using A only, work 2 rows st st.
Change to 2¼ mm needles.
Rep the 2 rib rows 4 times.
Cast off.

SLEEVES

Using 2¼ mm needles and A, cast on 49(57,57) sts.
Work 4 cm in rib as given for back.
Change to 3 mm needles.
For 1st and 2nd sizes only
Inc row: K10(14), * inc in next st, K9, rep from * to last 9(13) sts, inc in next st, K to end: 53(61) sts.
All sizes
Beg P(K,K) row, work 1(2,2) rows st st.
Increasing 1 st each end of next row, work 2 rows st st: 55(63,59) sts.
Now working in Spot patt as given for back and front, inc and work into patt 1 st each end of 3rd and every following 4th row until there are 83(91,91) sts.
Continuing in patt, work straight until sleeve measures approximately 18·5(21·5,24) cm from beg, ending with row 10 of patt.
Now work in patt as given for the first 6 rows of chart.
Cast off.

TO MAKE UP

Join shoulder seams for approximately 2·5 cm. Sew in sleeves, then join side and sleeve seams. Make 2 button loops either side of neck on front neck. Sew on buttons to back neck to correspond. Press lightly following instructions on ball band.

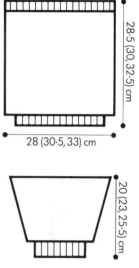

28·5 (30,32·5) cm

28 (30·5, 33) cm

20 (23, 25·5) cm

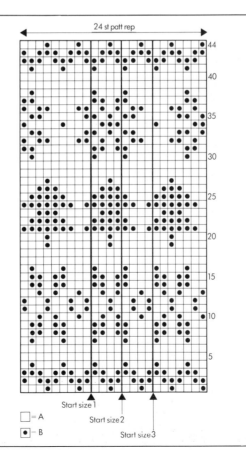

24 st patt rep

44
40
35
30
25
20
15
10
5

Start size 1
Start size 2
Start size 3

□ = A
▣ = B

This pretty little winter sweater has a band of Fair Isle pattern over the chest and shoulders, and a flurry of snowflakes over the body and arms.

KNITTING KNOW-HOW

MATERIALS AND EQUIPMENT

The materials and equipment required for hand-knitting are generally inexpensive to buy and light to carry – which is why knitters so often take their knitting around with them. The following is a list of the basics you are likely to need:

Knitting needles are the principal tool for hand-knitting and are generally sold in pairs (except for the larger sizes which can be bought separately), and in a wide variety of sizes. Gradually, all are being converted to metric sizing, and the numbers are indicated on the knob end of each needle. In metric sizes the larger the number shown, the larger the needle. They are generally made of plastic or coated metal, but the very large sizes, used for chunky yarns, may also be found in wood.

The size of the needles required varies with the thickness of the yarn and the finished effect that the knitter desires. The smaller the needle, the tighter the knitting, and the larger the needle the looser is the work. When experimenting with your own designs it is not necessary to confine yourself to the size of needle traditionally used for the chosen yarn, as exciting textures can be created by deviating from the recommended sizes.

Needles are also sold in different lengths, and the choice should be made according to whichever length feels the most comfortable for the knitter. They should be carefully stored in a dry, clean place so they do not become bent. Straight, clean needles facilitate even and fast knitting.

Circular needles are made with pointed plastic or coated metal sections on both ends of a flexible nylon section. They are also sold in different lengths and sizes, but care must be taken when deciding to use them so that the number of stitches easily reaches between the two pointed ends. They are simpler to use than sets of four needles, and a whole garment can be knitted on them, without seams to the armholes, especially when working plain knitting over a large number of stitches.

Double-pointed needles have points at both ends and are used usually in sets of four to knit circular items in the round, such as socks and sometimes neckbands.

Wool needles are specifically designed for sewing up. They have a large eye at one end for ease of threading yarns, and a blunt end to avoid splitting the yarn in the knitted pieces.

Stitch holders are generally used in the shaping of necklines. When it is necessary to reserve some

stitches from the body or the sleeves of the work, they are placed on a stitch holder until knitted into the main garment.

Needle gauges are usually plastic or metal frames with graduated holes which indicate the correct size of knitting needles.

READING KNITTING PATTERNS

CHOOSING THE YARN

Make sure the yarn you choose can be knitted up to the same tension as that of the pattern. Check the ball band or knit a sample tension square.

When buying yarn for a garment ensure that the whole quantity is from the one dye lot. Check the ball bands carefully as they will state both the colour number and dye lot number. Each dye lot differs in shade fractionally and there could be a marked line on the garment where the balls of different dye lots have been joined.

TENSION

The success of every knitted garment depends on using the correct tension, and you will never become a competent knitter until due consideration is given to this fact every time you commence a new piece of knitting. Tension does not simply mean even knitting, but indicates the number of stitches and rows over a given measurement, which is necessary to make the garment to the size as designed.

However experienced a knitter you are, it is essential to work a tension square in the stated yarn before commencing a pattern. Then at this stage you can assess if any adjustments need to be made in needle sizes or the design – before it is too late. The garment will only turn out to be the correct size if your tension is exactly the same as the one stated on the pattern.

Before starting a pattern, knit a tension square in the stated yarn and with the recommended needle size. Cast on a few more stitches than the figure given for the stitch tension and work a few more rows than the figure given for the row tension. Make sure that you knit in the stated stitch pattern as well.

When you have worked a square, lay it on a flat surface and mark out the suggested number of stitches and rows with pins. Do not start right at the edge stitch for these measurements. Now measure the distance between the pins. If you have too many stitches for the measurement, this means that your tension is too tight, and you should rework the square using a size larger needle. On the other hand if there are too few stitches, your tension is too loose, and a size smaller needle should be used to rework the tension square. It is necessary to continue experimenting with different needle sizes until the

Needle sizes

Metric	English	US
2mm	14	00
2¼mm	13	0
2¾mm	12	1
3mm	11	2
3¼mm	10	3
3¾mm	9	4
4mm	8	5
4½mm	7	6
5mm	6	7
5½mm	5	8
6mm	4	9
6½mm	3	10
7mm	2	10½
8mm	0	12
9mm	00	13
10mm	000	15

correct tension is achieved. You should also check the row tension at the same time, but it is easier to add a few rows to the depth of a garment, keeping the stitch pattern correct, than it is to adjust the width of a garment.

Another advantage of working a tension square is that it enables you to gain some experience with the stitch pattern used in your garment. It will speed up your work when you commence because you will be able to understand the terminology and abbreviations being used.

THE INSTRUCTIONS

After you have chosen the yarn and needles, and worked a tension square, it is time to commence the pattern. You will have already read the pattern with great care and marked the appropriate size you will be working. The pattern will indicate in which order the pieces are to be worked, and even though the choice may not be your own preference, it is advisable to stick to the order as printed. It is not uncommon to find instructions which relate to previously completed pieces for some necessary measurement. It is also advisable to join the pieces together in the order suggested because this may be relevant for some further work, such as neckbands or collars.

Try to make a habit of checking your work as you go along, especially if it is a complicated and repeated pattern. It is often easier for the eye to pick up a mistake during the course of a pattern than when the piece is completed. A careful check of the number of stitches is another indication that all is going according to plan. When you are checking the measurements of a piece of knitting do so on a flat surface and with a rigid measuring tape. Do not measure around curved edges, but place your tape measure at right-angles to a straight edge of the rows.

Where graphs or stitch diagrams are used it must be remembered that they only show the right side of the work, and that each graph square represents one stitch. Therefore, the odd-numbered rows, or front side, should be worked from right to left, and the even-numbered rows, or reverse side, should be worked from left to right. For left-handed knitters the patterns should be read in the reverse direction. When knitting on circular needles each round begins on the right-hand edge of each chart. Graphs are particularly popular with Fair Isle knitting and in collage or picture sweaters.

Another useful hint is to remember never to leave your knitting in the middle of a row, or if you have to leave the knitting for any length of time do not leave it in the middle of a piece. You will discover, when you recommence, an ugly ridge across the row where you stopped knitting, and it is virtually impossible to remove it.

When knitting in rows try, wherever possible, to join new balls in at the end of a row, as a knot in the middle of a row of knitting will only result in an unsightly hole. If it is unavoidable to have a mid-row join, and when knitting using circle needles, join the yarns by splicing the ends together as described on page 133.

ABBREVIATIONS

The accompanying list of abbreviations needs to be studied carefully to enable you to use the section of knitting patterns. In some of the patterns there are extra abbreviations that are relevant only to that particular pattern; in such cases these are explained at the beginning of the pattern.

K	knit
P	purl
st(s)	stitch(es)
st st	stocking stitch (1 row K, 1 row P)
rev st st	reversed stocking stitch (1 row P, 1 row K)
patt	pattern
rep	repeat
beg	beginning
inc	increase(ing)
dec	decrease(ing)
in	inches
cm	centimetres
mm	millimetres
g st	garter stitch (every row K)
sl	slip
tog	together
psso	pass slipped stitch over
skpo	slip 1, knit 1, pass slipped stitch over
tbl	through back of loop
yrn	yarn round needle
yon	yarn over needle
Yf	yarn forward
Yb	yarn back
pw	purlwise
kw	knitwise
M1	Make one worked as follows: pick up bar between stitch just worked and next stitch on left-hand needle and knit into back of it.
sl 1 pw	slip one purlwise
ytb	yarn to back
ytf	yarn to front
ch	chain
dc	double crochet

BASIC SKILLS

Before attempting to knit any garment, it is necessary to master a few basic knitting techniques and stitches. It is advisable to practise with any scraps of yarn so as to feel confident when tackling a pattern, and to feel comfortable using the correct equipment.

The basics of learning to knit are very simple – casting on, casting off, increasing and decreasing, and the two elementary stitches of knit and purl. Most patterns consist of differing combinations of these two stitches.

The most common method of casting on and casting off is the two-needle method. Casting off may be done on a knit or a purl row, or even across a ribbed band.

CASTING ON

1. Make a single loop (leaving a short length of yarn for finishing off) and place it on the left-hand needle. Insert the right-hand needle through the loop on the left-hand needle, from front to back. Holding the yarn at the back of the needles, pass it under and over the point of the right-hand needle.

2. Draw the loop through the stitch on the left-hand needle to the front of the work and place it onto the left-hand needle.

3. Place the right-hand needle between the first two stitches, pass yarn under and over as before, draw yarn through and put it on the left-hand needle.

4. Continue making stitches in this way until the correct number have been cast on to the left-hand needle.

THE KNIT STITCH

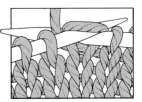

1. Hold the needle with the stitches to be knitted in the left hand with the yarn at the back of the work.

2. Put the right-hand needle through the first stitch, take the yarn under and over the end of the right-hand needle.

3. Pull the new loop on the right-hand needle through the work to the front and slip original stitch off the left-hand needle.

Beginning a new row
When the end of the first row is reached, all the stitches should be on the right-hand needle. Transfer this needle to the left hand ready to commence the second row, and use the empty needle to knit with in the right hand.

THE PURL STITCH

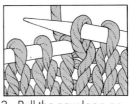

1. Hold the stitches to be purled in the left hand with the yarn at the front of the work.

2. Put the right-hand needle through the front of the first stitch, pass the yarn over and around right-hand needle from right to left.

3. Pull the new loop through the stitch and slip it from the left hand needle, and so the new stitch will remain on the right-hand needle.

Changing from knit to purl
After completing the knit stitch bring the yarn through to the front of the work between the needles. Then purl the next stitch in the usual way.

JOINING YARN

It is best to try not to run out of yarn in the middle of a row, as the joining knot will be evident from the front of the work. If it is unavoidable, use the following method to join the yarn. Unravel short ends of the two pieces of yarn, and overlap half the strands from each piece. Twist them together firmly. Cut the remaining threads. The method is known as 'splicing' the yarn.

Top is a photograph of stocking stitch as viewed from the front of the work. One row is plain and the next is purled and this combination is continued. The right side is smooth and the back is ridged as in the second photograph. When this side of stocking stitch is used as the right side of the work, it is known as reversed stocking stitch. When every row is knitted or every row is purled the stitch is known as garter stitch.

PICKING UP DROPPED STITCHES

When a dropped stitch occurs a little patience will overcome the problem. It is not necessary to pull out the needle and undo several rows. Picking up is easily done on a simple stitch pattern, but much more difficult in the course of a complicated pattern. When it occurs in a pattern, and after you have rectified the problem, always check that the number of stitches is correct before continuing with the work. To pick up a dropped stitch the only equipment you need to use is a crochet hook.

THE MOSS STITCH

This stitch is one of the more basic stitches and is often used to fill in between pattern panels or as a border. The first row is worked by alternately knitting one stitch, then purling the next. On the next row, if the first stitch facing you is a plain stitch (the smooth side of the stitch) then it is worked as a purl stitch. If it is a purl stitch facing you (with the ridge standing out from the knitting) then it is worked as a knit stitch. All following rows are worked in this way, making sure that the stitches form the alternating knit and purl pattern going up as well as across the rows.

Picking up a knit stitch

With the right side facing insert the hook through dropped stitch from front to back. Place the hook around the thread immediately above the dropped stitch and pull the thread through the stitch. Do this until the same level is reached as the rest of the work and place the stitch on the left-hand needle.

Picking up a purl stitch

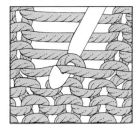

With the wrong side facing, put the hook through the dropped stitch from back to front. Place the hook around the thread immediately in front and draw through the dropped stitch. Continue until the same level is reached as the rest of the work and place the stitch on the left-hand needle.

UNPICKING MISTAKES

In the course of intricate pattern work, occasionally the number of stitches may vary from the original number. It is necessary to keep a careful check on the number of stitches so as not to throw out the whole pattern.

When a mistake is discovered, careful unpicking is the best way to rectify the error. If this is done stitch by stitch, taking care not to twist the stitches, no evidence of the unpicking will remain.

Unpicking knit stitches   **Unpicking purl stitches**

Put left-hand needle through lower stitch. Pull right-hand needle out of the stitch above it and pull the yarn out with the right hand.

With yarn at front on purl side, put left-hand needle in lower stitch, pull right-hand needle out of the stitch above and pull out yarn.

CASTING OFF

Follow the pattern as to which of three methods should be used for casting off. If no indication is given, cast off knitwise. Take care to have an even edge, because if it is too tight the edge will pucker. On most neck edges it is advisable to cast off with a right-hand needle that is one size larger than those used for working the body of the neckband. This will give the neckline more elasticity.

Casting off knitwise

Knit the first two stitches. Put the end of left-hand needle into the front of the first stitch, lift it over second stitch and off the

needle. Knit another stitch and repeat process until one stitch remains. Break the yarn and draw it firmly through the last stitch.

Casting off purlwise and in rib

To cast off purlwise, purl the first two stitches, and lift the first stitch over the second and off the needle. Continue purling and casting off to the last stitch and fasten off the broken yarn. For a ribbed casting off (i.e. over K1, P1 rib), as used on most neck and arm

bands, knit the first stitch, then purl the second. Lift the first stitch over the second and off the needle. Knit the third stitch and lift the second over. Continue in this manner until all the stitches are cast off. Fasten off the last stitch with the end of the yarn.

SHAPING

Nearly every knitted garment includes some shaping, either for sleeves or necklines, or in the basic body shape. Shaping is done by either increasing or decreasing stitches or by a combination of both. Where the object is solely to shape a garment these techniques can be worked almost invisibly. However, they can also be used in a decorative way to create lacy and embossed stitch patterns.

DECREASING

This is the main method used to reduce the width of garments, especially for sleeve top and armhole shaping, and at the neckline. It is also the basis for many intricate, but decorative stitch patterns. Always use the decreasing method that is given in the pattern. If no method is given, then use the 'knit two together' method.

Knitting two stitches together

Put the right-hand needle into front of second stitch and then front of first stitch, knitwise. Yarn around

needle and pull through both stitches and drop both stitches off left-hand needle.

Purling two stitches together

With yarn at front, put right-hand needle into the front of the first and then the second stitch, purlwise. Wind the yarn

around the needle, and pull it through both the stitches, then drop them both off the left-hand needle at the same time.

Slipstitch decreasing, knitwise

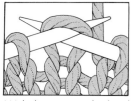

With the yarn at the back of the work, slip the first stitch from the left- to the right-hand needle, knitwise. Do not knit it. Now knit the second stitch. With the left-hand

needle, lift the first stitch over the second knitted stitch and off the needle. In patterns this is referred to as slip 1, knit 1, pass slip stitch over.

INCREASING STITCHES

The second most commonly used method of shaping knitted garments is by increasing the number of stitches, and it is also used extensively in intricate pattern designs, especially for lacy stitches. There are several methods of increasing stitches but the two most often used are the invisible and the decorative methods.

Invisible increasing

This is the simplest method of increasing. It is generally used to change the shape of a garment at the sides, but can be worked anywhere along a row just as successfully.

Two stitches from one knitwise

Knit into the front of the next stitch with the right-hand needle, but do not slip it off the left-hand needle. Now knit into the

back of the same stitch with right-hand needle, and slip the stitch off left-hand needle making two from one.

Two stitches from one purlwise

Purl into the front of next stitch but do not slip it off the left-hand needle. With right-hand needle

purl into the back of this stitch again and then slip it off the left-hand needle.

Knitting into running thread between knitwise

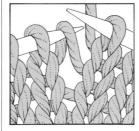

With the left-hand needle pick up the loop which lies in front of it and keep it on the left-hand needle.

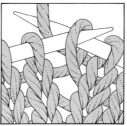

Knit into the back of this loop

Slip it off the left-hand needle. This method is sometimes called 'make one'.

Knitting into running thread between purlwise

With the left-hand needle pick up the loop which lies in front of it and keep it on the left-hand needle.

Purl into the back of this loop.

Slip it off the left-hand needle.

Decorative increasing

In some patterns the increased stitch is featured as a decorative item, by creating a small hole with every increased stitch. The increased stitch is formed between two existing stitches by looping the yarn over the needle.

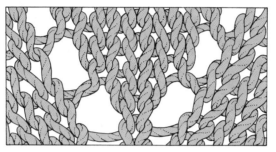

Yarn forward

To make a new stitch between two knit stitches, put the yarn in front. Put right-hand needle into next stitch knitwise. Pass yarn over

right-hand needle, under the tip of left-hand one, and around and under the tip of the right-hand needle again. Pull the loop through and slip

stitch from left-hand needle. On the next row, in stocking stitch, purl into this new loop as usual.

Yarn around needle

To make a new stitch between two purl stitches, begin with the yarn at the front of the work, loop it around the right-hand needle and back to the front. Now purl the next stitch normally and pull off the

left-hand needle. On the next row, in stocking stitch, knit into the new loop as usual. To make a stitch between a purl and a knit stitch, take the yarn from front over the needle to knit the next stitch, called 'yarn over

needle'. To make a stitch between a knit and a purl stitch, bring the yarn to the front, then back over the needle to the front again ready to purl the next stitch, called 'yarn forward and over needle'.

ADVANCED TECHNIQUES

The following techniques require a little more skill than those already covered, but they are not difficult to acquire as they incorporate the basic stitches that have already been learnt.

Simple bobbles and cables are the basic design elements of many complicated patterns, but in themselves they are not difficult to master.

It is also necessary to learn colourwork techniques, even if you only want to use one additional colour. Next come instructions for making buttonholes, as these are invariably found on cardigans, jackets and waistcoats.

Lastly, it is also necessary to learn how to pick up stitches along the edges of knitting in order to form collars and armholes.

CABLE

All forms of cable are worked on the principle of moving a number of stitches from one place to another in the same row. Up to two stitches at a time can be moved quite easily, using only two knitting needles, but when it is necessary to transfer more than this number, it is easier to use a short, double-pointed cable needle. The stitches to be moved are held on the cable needle, either at the front or the back of the work, until needed.

Simple cable knitwise

Take the right-hand needle around the back of the first stitch on the left-hand needle, and knit into the back of the

second stitch. Then knit into the front of the first stitch and slip both stitches off the left-hand needle together.

Simple cable purlwise

Take the right-hand needle in front of the first stitch on the left-hand needle and purl into the front of the second stitch.

Then purl into the front of the first stitch and slip both stitches off the left-hand needle at the same time.

Cabling with a cable needle

Cable twist to left: slip two stitches onto a cable needle and put at the front of the work. Knit the next two stitches and then knit the two stitches from the cable needle.

Cable twist to right: slip two stitches onto a cable needle and put at the back of the work. Knit

the next two stitches and then knit the two stitches from the cable needle.

BOBBLES

The basis for making bobbles is always to make more than one stitch from the stitch where the bobble is desired, and then decrease back to the original stitch in the same or a later row.

To make a bobble

Knit to the position where the bobble is required. Make five stitches from the next stitch by knitting into the front then back of the stitch twice, and then knit into the front again. Turn and purl these five stitches, turn and knit the five stitches. With the left-hand needle lift second, third, fourth and fifth stitches over the first stitch and off the right-hand needle. Knit to position of next bobble and repeat.

PICKING UP STITCHES

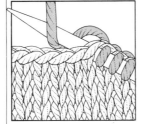

Picking up on the cast off edge

Push the right-hand needle through the first edge stitch. Take the yarn under and over the needle and make a knit stitch. Continue making knit stitches in each stitch until right number exists.

Picking up on the selvedge

Working with the right-hand needle, put it through the fabric between the first two rows and form a knit stitch. Continue making knit stitches between every two rows.

BUTTONHOLES

Many patterns require buttonholes to be made. The two main methods are horizontal and vertical buttonholes used on the bands of jackets and cardigans. When small buttonholes are needed, such as on lightweight clothing, simple eyelet holes are ideal as they are neat and unobtrusive.

Horizontal buttonholes

Knit to the position of the buttonhole and cast off the required number of stitches to fit the button size. Continue to the end of the row. On the next row, work to the stitch before the casting off, knit into it twice and then cast on one less number of stitches than were cast off on the row before. Continue working until the position of the next buttonhole is reached, and then repeat the process.

Vertical buttonholes

Knit to the position of the buttonhole and then divide the work and knit each side separately. When each side is long enough to fit the button comfortably, continue to work across the whole row. Continue working until the position of the next buttonhole is reached and then repeat the whole process.

Eyelet buttonholes

See over page

To make eyelet buttonholes

Work to the position of the buttonhole. Bring the yarn forward between the needles to the front of the work and take it over the needle to knit the next two stitches together.

On the next row, purl the yarn taken over. To make a channel for threading ribbon or cord, work a succession of eyelets across the row at the point where a channel is required.

BUTTON LOOPS

These loops are one of the simpler methods of placing buttonholes on a knitted garment.

Start by threading a needle with yarn in the required colour, then join to the edge of the garment, in the position that the button loop is required, by taking a few small stitches.

Take the needle a little further along the edge, just under the width of the button, and make a small stitch leaving a loop large enough to go over the button. Insert the needle back through the fabric at the original place and take another small stitch. Repeat this several times so that there are four or five thicknesses of thread for the loop.

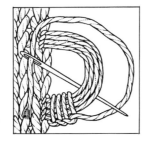

Finishing off

Neatly work buttonhole stitch over all of the threads to completely cover the loop.

COLOURWORK

Modern hand-knitting uses a great deal of colourwork, either to emphasize a pattern or in careful blending of colours, and in collage and graph knitting. Picture sweaters which incorporate several colours in the body of the work are especially popular.

Although it may at first appear difficult to handle two or more balls of yarn at the same time, once stranding and weaving of colours has been mastered, the problem quickly disappears. Stranding is usually used if the pattern is small with only three or four stitches worked in each colour. If there are more than five stitches at a time in one colour, it is better to use the weaving technique so that long loops are not left on the back of the knitting to become pulled.

Joining in new colours

New colours can be joined in at the beginning of or during a row of knitting. It needs to be done smoothly and securely, so that no holes result where there is a join, especially in the middle of a knitted piece.

At the beginning of a row

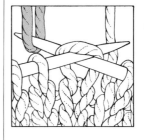

Put the right-hand needle into the first stitch and with the first colour make a loop and then make one with the new colour over this needle. Finish the stitch by pulling these loops through in the normal way. To make more secure, work the next two stitches with both ends of the new yarn. At the end of the next row be careful to work the last three stitches as single stitches.

In the centre of a row

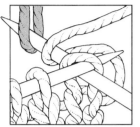

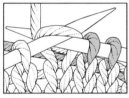

Knit to the position where the new colour is to be introduced. Put

right-hand needle into the next stitch and with the new colour make a loop around the end of this needle. Make the stitch in the normal way, but work the next two stitches with both ends of the new yarn. When working the next row remember to work these as single stitches.

Stranding colours

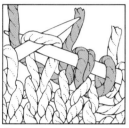

After joining in the new colour in one of the above methods, work

with the first colour and loosely carry the new yarn across the back of the work until it is needed. Change to the new colour and strand the first colour across the back until it is needed once more.

Weaving colours knitwise

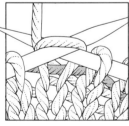

When the contrast yarn is carried across more than five stitches it must be woven into the back of the work. Keep first colour in the right hand and second in the left. Knit the first stitch in the usual way, but on the

second and every alternate stitch put the right-hand needle into the stitch, loop the left-hand yarn across top of the needle, then work the stitch in the normal way with the first colour.

Weaving colours purlwise

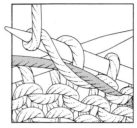

On the purl side, weave the colours alternately over and under every stitch. Weave it over by inserting the needle into the next stitch, pass the yarn to be woven over the top of the needle, then purl the stitch with

the first colour in the normal way. On the next stitch weave the yarn under the stitch, by keeping the woven yarn pulled taut with the left hand whilst purling the stitch in the normal way with the first colour.

SWISS DARNING

Swiss darning is a simple technique, using a contrast coloured yarn to embroider the surface of plain stocking stitch by imitating and covering each knitted stitch with the contrast yarn. Providing it is worked stitch by stitch, without pulling the yarn too tightly, it is almost impossible to tell that it has not been knitted by using the motif knitting technique. Whenever coloured motifs are used within knitting, it is nearly always possible to work the whole section of knitting in one colour only, then to Swiss-darn the motifs on before making up.

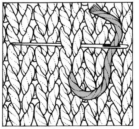

1. Thread a needle with contrast yarn and fasten at back of work. Bring needle through to front of work, through the centre of the stitch below the stitch to be covered. Insert the needle through the knitted fabric, under the stitch in the row above and draw the yarn lightly through.

2. Insert the needle back through the fabric at the base of the embroidered stitch. Repeat steps 1 and 2 as necessary to form the motif.

WORKING FROM CHARTS

Normally a chart is given in a knitting pattern when it would be too complicated to give out the pattern row by row. Sometimes a chart is given to show where different stitch patterns must be worked, but usually they are used for colour patterns and motifs which are worked in stocking stitch. When reading a chart one square represents one stitch to be knitted and one row to be worked.

If the design is an all-over pattern, the yarn not in use can generally be stranded or woven in across the back of the work, but if there are large areas of one colour, use a separate ball for each block of colour. To avoid holes in the work join each section of colour together by twisting the yarns together on the wrong side of the work every time you change colour.

On a knit row   **On a purl row**

Knit in first yarn to position for changing colour. Keeping yarns at back of work, place the first colour over top of the second colour, then pick up the second colour and knit to the next colour change.

On a purl row, work as for a knit row except keeping yarns at front of work and always twisting yarns together when changing colour.

FINISHING OFF

The finishing and sewing together of a knitted garment is often thought to be tedious, but a little care taken at this stage will make all the difference to the success of the finished garment. The loose ends of the wool, at either side of the knitting, should be darned into the back of the work with a wool needle. Then trim the yarn close to the fabric.

Before deciding whether to press the work, it is necessary to read the ball bands carefully to see if the yarn is suitable for pressing. Here you will also find advice as to the correct temperature for pressing. Pressing is not recommended on textured work, mohair, or any ribbed bands.

Turn the piece right side down on a padded surface. Pin the edges to the correct shape, also checking the measurements. Cover the knitting with a damp cloth. Lower the iron, but do not pull it across the fabric. Lift the iron and lower it gently onto another section.

SEWING UP

Follow the pattern carefully as to the order in which the pieces should be sewn together, as this may be relevant to any further work, such as neckbands or collars. The two main methods of joining the edges are with an invisible seam or a back stitch seam. The latter is the stronger seam and is best when working against the grain of the fabric. When sleeves are sewn in, the stitches should not be so tight that there is no room for stretching.

Invisible seam   **Back stitch seam**

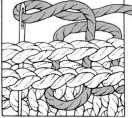

With right sides of the fabric facing, match the edges. Secure the yarn at the bottom of the seam. The needle must be passed under the thread between the first two edge stitches. Now pick up the next thread on the opposite side and firmly draw the two edges together, without any puckering. Continue along the seam.

With right sides together, match the edges. Secure the yarn at the bottom. Work from right to left over one knitted stitch at a time. Take yarn across one stitch at the back and through to front. Take yarn back to the right by one stitch through to the back, to the left by two stitches and to the front. Continue till the seam is complete.

GRAFTING

An alternative method to casting off and then sewing the edges together, such as shoulder seams, is to graft them. In order to do this the stitches, which are normally cast off, must be left on a spare needle or holder until the pattern tells you to join that seam. A grafted seam is ideal for baby clothes because, as well as being totally invisible, there are no hard ridges of knitting, which is found by the two edges being sewn together.

To Work the Grafted Seam

Leave the stitches that are to be joined as a seam on a holder, or waste yarn, until needed.

Place the two pieces to be joined on a flat surface, with right sides facing upwards, and with the two sets of stitches opposite each other.

Thread a needle with a length of yarn approximately four times the length of the seam.

Fasten the yarn to one edge and bring the needle up through the first stitch on one of the pieces of knitting.

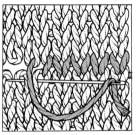

Take the needle across to the other set of stitches and down through the first stitch, then back up through the second stitch. Bring the needle back across to the first set of stitches and down through the first stitch then back up through the second stitch. Now take it back to the second set of stitches and down through the second stitch then up through the third stitch. Continue until the end is reached. Fasten off.

POMPOMS

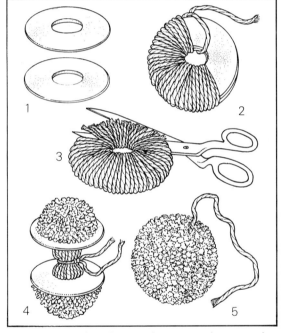

1. Cut two circles of cardboard to the diameter required for the pompom. Cut a smaller circle out of the centre of each one, about a third of the total diameter.
2. Hold the two rings together, wind the yarn round and round the rings until the centre hole is almost filled.
3. Inserting the blade of the scissors between the edges of the two rings, cut through the yarn round the edge.
4. Gently pull the rings apart and using an odd piece of yarn, tie it tightly round the centre of the pompom and fasten off securely.
5. Pull the cardboard rings off of the pompom, and fluff up into shape.

AFTER-CARE

Washing Always use warm, never hot, water and a washing detergent specially manufactured for cleaning knitwear. Do not soak hand-knitted garments, and avoid the need for this with frequent and brief washes. When wet, never lift the garment by the shoulders, as it is very easy for the weight to distort the shape. In the final rinse water, add fabric conditioner, so that the natural pile of the yarn is released. After all the soap has been removed by rinsing, gently squeeze out the excess water.

Drying This should be done on a flat surface, away from direct heat and sunlight. Ideally, place the wet garment on a newspaper which has been covered by a thick, clean towel. Pat out any creases and leave until dry. A final airing will be necessary, preferably on an outdoor clothes line. To prevent peg marks on a garment, thread a clean pair of nylon tights through the two sleeves and neck, and peg the tights onto the line.

Pressing If the washing and drying have been carried out carefully, pressing should not be necessary. If it is still thought desirable check the ball band for the correct temperature setting for the iron, and follow the same instructions for pressing as given for the making-up of a garment.

Wear and tear The two most common signs of wear and tear are small balls of fibre forming on the surface of a garment and snagging. The small balls can be removed with a specially designed comb which can be bought from a haberdashery department. To remove snags use a blunt-ended needle and pull the snag through to the reverse side. Gently adjust the stitch to its original shape and size and knot the end at the back.

LAUNDRY SYMBOLS

The wash tub indicates suitability for washing and the correct water temperatures. The upper figure indicates the automatic washing cycle which is suitable for machine washable yarns. The lower figure indicates the water temperature for hand washing. If the yarn is only suitable for hand washing a hand will be shown in the tub, and if the tub is crossed through the yarn is then only suitable for dry cleaning.

When bleach can be used a triangle with the letters CL inside will appear, but generally the triangle will be crossed out as most yarns cannot be bleached. Suitable ironing temperatures are shown by an iron containing three dots for hot, two for warm, and one dot for a cool iron. An iron crossed out indicates that pressing is not recommended.

Extreme care should be given to a garment knitted with a mixture of yarns whether of different types or weights, and the lowest temperature shown on the ball bands should be used.

For dry cleaning a circle appears with the letters A, P and F, which refer to the different dry cleaning solvents. A crossed out circle indicates that the garment cannot be dry cleaned.

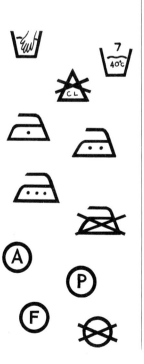

YARN SPINNERS AND STOCKISTS

BERGER DU NORD

Australia
Woolcraft Pty Ltd
16 The Mall
3081 West Heidelberg
Victoria

Canada
Berger du Nord
9697 St Laurent
Montreal
Quebec N3L 2N1

France
Berger du Nord
50 Rue de L'Epideme
Tourcoing

United Kingdom
Viking Wools Ltd
Rothay Holme
Ambleside
Cumbria LA22 0HQ

United States of America
Brookman & Son Ltd
4416 North East Eleventh
    Avenue
334 Fort Lauderdale
Florida 33334

JAEGER
(see Patons)

KING COLE

Canada
Mrs V Hobkirk
RR3
Prescott
Ontario K0E 1T0

United Kingdom
King Cole Ltd
Merrie Mills
Old Souls Way
Bingley
Bradford BD16 2AX

United States of America
Mrs Maureen McClellan
1811 Altavista Avenue
Escondido
California 92027

Jane Simpson Cohen
Passap Knitting Machine
    Center
7385 Pacific Street
Omaha NE68124

Robin & Russ Handweavers
533 North Adams Street
McMinnville
Oregon 97128

Carol A Taylor
Exquisicat Imports
PO Box 6321
Richmond
Virginia 2320

PATONS

Australia
Coats & Patons (Australia) Ltd
321–355 Fern Tree Gully Road
PO Box 110
Mount Waverley
Victoria 3149

Canada
Patons & Baldwins (Canada) Ltd
1001 Rose Lawn Avenue
Toronto
Ontario

France
Denys Frys Freres SA
89 Rue de Tourcoing, BP 34
59960 Neuville-en-Ferrain

Germany
Seiden & Garn GmbH
Hochdorf Abrichstr 4
Postfach 1160
7800 Freiburg/Breisgau

Holland
Nomotta Breigarens BV
Sterrenbergweg 42a
3768 BT Soesterberg

New Zealand
Coats Patons (New Zealand)
263 Ti Rakau Drive
Pakuranga
Auckland

United Kingdom
Patons & Baldwins Ltd
PO Box Darlington
County Durham DL1 1YQ

United States of America
Susan Bates Inc
212 Middlesex Avenue
Route 9A
Connecticut 06412

PHILDAR

Canada
Phildar Ltee
6200 Est
Bd H Bourassa
Montreal Nord H1G 5X3

France
Phildar DME
Centre Mercure
445 Boulevard Gambetta
59977 Tourcoing Cedex

Germany
Phildar Wolle GmbH
Ostring 6
Postfach 4627
6200 Wiesbaden-Nordenstadt

Holland
Phildar BV
Bukkumweg 11
Postbus 72
5081 – CT Hilvarenbeek

United Kingdom
Phildar (UK) Ltd
4 Gambrel Road
Westgate Industrial Estate
Northampton NN5 5NF

United States of America
Phildar Inc
6438 Dawson Boulevard
85 North
Norcross
Georgia 30093

PINGOUIN

Australia
C P Sullivan Pty Ltd
47–57 Collins Street
Alexandria
New South Wales

Canada
Promafil Canada Ltd
300 Boulevard Laurentien
Suite 100
St Lauren
Quebec H4M 2L4

Germany
AFRA – GmbH
Grevenweg 89
D 2000
Hamburg 26

Holland
M Yvo van der Velden
Hildo Kropstraat 8A
NL
3431 CC Nieuwegein

Norway
Skaug and Nielsen Als
Postboks 40
N 1472 Fjellhamar

Sweden
Daftas A/S Svenk Filial
Adolf Fredriks Kyrkogata 12
3 van TR S
11137 Stockholm

United Kingdom
French Wools Ltd
7–11 Lexington Street
London W1

United States of America
Pingouin Corporation
PO Box 100
Highway 45
James Town
South Carolina 29453

ROWAN

Australia
Sunspun Enterprises
195 Canterbury Road
Canterbury 3126

Canada
Estelle
39 Continental Place
Scarborough
Ontario M1R 2T4

United Kingdom
Green Lane Mill
Washpit
Homfirth
West Yorkshire HD7 1RW

United States of America
Westminster Trading
   Corporation
5 Northern Boulevard
Amhurst
New Hampshire 03031

SCHAFFHAUSER

Australia
Jaipark Pty Ltd
PO Box 576
Chatswood 2067

Canada
White Knitting Products
1470 Birchmont Road
Scarborough
Ontario M1P 261

White Knitting Products
1302 Stewardson Way
New Westminster B C
V3M 4N4

Europe
Schaffhauser Wolle
Schoeller Albers AG
Ebnatstrasse 65
CH 8201 Schaffhausen
Switzerland

New Zealand
Warnaar Trading Co Ltd
PO Box 19561
374 Ferry Road
Christchurch

United Kingdom
Woolgatherers
10 Barley Mow Passage
Chiswick
London W4 4PH

United States of America
Qualitat Ltd
Benaroya Business Park
Building 3
3498 N W Yeon
Portland OR 97210

SIRDAR

Australia
Sirdar (Australia) Pty Ltd
PO Box 110
Mt Waverley
Victoria 3149

Canada
Diamond Yard
153 Bridgeland Avenue
Unit 11
Toronto
Ontario M6A 2Y6

New Zealand
Alliance Textiles
PO Box 716
Dunedin

Norway
A S Knapphuset
PO Box 100
N-5095 Ulset

Garnguiden AS
N-1900 Fetsund

Sweden
Curt U
Bergvall Textil AB
Brankyrkagatan
S-117 Stockholm

United Kingdom
Sirdar PLC
Flanshaw Lane
Alverthorpe
Wakefield
West Yorkshire WF2 9ND

United States of America
Kendex Corporation
31332 Via Colinas 107
Westlake Village
California 91362

TWILLEYS

United Kingdom
H G Twilley Ltd
Hand-knitting Yarns
Roman Mill
Stamford
Lincolnshire PE9 1BG

United States of America
Rainbow Gallery
13615 Victory Boulevard
Suite 245 Van Nuys
California 91401

Gemini
720 East Jericho Turnpike
Huntingdon Station
New York 11746

WOOLGATHERERS

Australia
Mail order service available
from UK address below

Canada
As Australia

France
Bouton d'Or
Pierre de Loye & Cie
Rue de la Concorde
84100 Orange

United Kingdom
Woolgatherers
10 Barley Mow Passage
Chiswick
London W4 4PH

United States of America
As Australia

YARNWORKS

United Kingdom
YarnWorks Ltd
Waring and Gillow Building
Western Avenue
London W3

United States of America
Tanglewool
57 Church Street
Lenox
MA 01240

Coulter Studio
118E Square Street
NY 10022

The Knitting Basket
5812 Grove Avenue
Richmond
Virginia 23226

Where particular yarns are not
available locally, details of
nearest suppliers may be
obtained from the companies
listed here.

ACKNOWLEDGEMENTS

Editor Isabel Papadakis
Art Editor/Design Pat Sumner
Assisted by Brazzle Atkins
Production Controller Maryann Rogers
Pattern Editor Sue Hopper

Photography Fiona Alison
Styling Amanda Cooke, Hilary Guy, Vicky Wood
Illustrations Jeremy Firth, Coral Mula, Lindsay Blow

The publishers would like to thank the following for supplying clothes and props for photography:
Benetton (0–12)
H and M Hennes
Klimages
Lott 32, Camden, NW1
The London Toy and Model Museum
The Pet Shop, Harlsden, NW10
The Pine Mine, Wandsworth, SW6
Ravel
Rosemary Smith, handmade buttons on pages 18, 37, 70 and 129
Villeroy and Boch

The Teddy Bears photographed are British made by Merrythought and are available from most good toy shops and department stores.

The verse on page 98 is from 'Furry Bear', *Now We are Six*, by A.A. Milne, Methuen Paperbacks.

The Publishers would also like to thank Tessa for all her hard work and productivity, the additional designers, and all the knitters including Mrs Edna Booth, Mrs Margaret Burgess, Mrs Vera Jones and, in particular, Mrs Gina Watts-Russell.